They Had No Voice

To: Senator Jeff Clemens,
Friend and great
legislator, Best
wishes.
Denny

THEY HAD NO VOICE

My Fight for Alabama's Forgotten Children

BY DENNY ABBOTT

WITH DOUGLAS KALAJIAN

FOREWORD BY JOHN WALSH

NEWSOUTH BOOKS
Montgomery

NewSouth Books
105 S. Court Street
Montgomery, AL 36104

Copyright © 2013 by Denny Abbott
All rights reserved under International and Pan-American Copyright
Conventions. Published in the United States by NewSouth Books,
a division of NewSouth, Inc., Montgomery, Alabama.

Library of Congress Cataloging-in-Publication Data

Abbott, Denny.
They had no voice : my fight for Alabama's forgotten children /
by Denny Abbott, with Douglas Kalajian ; foreword by John Walsh.

pages cm

ISBN-13: 978-1-60306-209-1
ISBN-10: 1-60306-209-2

1. Abbott, Denny. 2. African American juvenile delinquents—Alabama—
Montgomery. 3. Juvenile delinquents—Abuse of—Alabama—Montgomery.
4. Juvenile detention—Alabama—Montgomery. 5. Juvenile corrections—
Alabama—Montgomery. I. Kalajian, Douglas. II. Title.
HV9106.M66A23 2013
364.36092—dc23
[B]

2013001543

Printed in the United States of America
by Versa Press

To my wife, Adele, who inspired me to write this book, and to my children, Court, Kim, and Drew, the best a parent could ever hope for.

And to John Walsh, the best child advocate this country has ever seen.

The ultimate measure of a man is not where he stands in moments of comfort and convenience, but where he stands at times of challenge and controversy.

— MARTIN LUTHER KING JR., in *Strength to Love*

Contents

Foreword

John Walsh

I have known Denny Abbott for nearly three decades. We've worked together, traveling all over the country in our quest to improve the resources regarding missing and exploited children, and worked on developing and improving legislation as well as keeping the public informed. From the start, I have always understood that his tenacity in the service of righting what he sees as wrong was almost without equal; I have seen him in action, how hard he works, how uncompromising he always was in our efforts together.

We first began to work together after my wife, Revé, and I announced, in the aftermath of the discovery that our son, Adam, had been murdered, that we wanted to set up a nonprofit group that would focus on the tragedy of missing and exploited children. Denny had been working with a group that wanted to expand to serve that same need and offered an established organization with experience that would give us a fine foundation. So, in 1982, Revé and I joined the board of directors of the group, and its name, Child Advocacy, Inc., was changed to the Adam Walsh Child Resource Center, Inc. Denny became the national director of the new organization.

The center, with six offices in four states—California, Florida, New York, and Ohio—kept us very busy. We traveled around the country, speaking to legislative groups and others about the need for legislative reform that would provide more protection for children. This led us into all kinds of interesting research and into drafting model legislation that would address the problems that surfaced in our research. Ultimately, the Adam Walsh Center merged with the National Center for Missing and Exploited Children, based in Washington, D.C.

While I had some awareness of Denny's fight for the rights of black children in detention in Alabama in the 1960s and early 1970s, and knew he had sued the state and been fired for his efforts—that he had been willing to suffer for his beliefs—I did not know the whole story. I encouraged him in his efforts to tell his story for two reasons. First, it's a good story, and I wanted to know the details and thought others would find the story interesting, too. Second, the world needs stories like Denny's, now more than ever. We need to brighten fading ideals and establish new models of true public service and strong character. We need the details of costs and rewards, the facts of the process that prove that one person can stand up for what is right and help abolish what is wrong.

John Walsh *is the founder and leader of the national movement to protect missing and exploited children. He is also well-known as the longtime host of* America's Most Wanted.

Introduction

When I was a young man in the 1960s, it was my job to deliver black children to a slave camp on the outskirts of Montgomery, Alabama.

I want to make it clear from the start that I'm not using the word "slave" as a figure of speech, and I'm not exaggerating for dramatic effect. I'm talking about a place where children as young as twelve were held by brute force and put to hard labor in the fields. They were worked until they dropped, and when they dropped they were beaten with sticks. Often they were beaten for no reason at all, and sometimes they were forced to have sex with the men who beat them.

The most horrifying fact about this place is that it was run by the State of Alabama.

Its formal name was the Alabama Industrial School for Negro Children at Mt. Meigs. I was a probation officer for the Montgomery County Family Court, a "boy's counselor," as the job was euphemistically titled. My duties included transporting juvenile offenders from the detention center in downtown Montgomery to this so-called reform school, which wasn't much of a school at all and was in far greater need of reform than the kids who were sent there.

I truly had no idea just how awful that place was at first. I was only twenty-one when I got the job, just three years ahead of the oldest boys in my charge, and I was probably a little slow to catch on because the children who returned to Montgomery after serving a term at Mt. Meigs were unlikely to confide their fears and misery to a white man who carried a badge and handcuffs.

But over the years, I heard enough and saw enough and sensed enough about Mt. Meigs to understand that it was a place out of time run by people who were out of control. I tried, time and again, to do something about it. For a long time, I did what civil servants are trained to do: I filed reports. I wrote up every detail of every complaint that came my way and I sent them to all the right people. Every one of those reports came back with the same reply: "Complaint unfounded." I was always disappointed, but I was never surprised. The simple truth was that nobody in a position of authority cared if black children were being abused, even if the abusers were the very people sworn to protect them.

At least I was doing something, or trying to. This is what I told myself. I might have kept on telling myself that if the five bravest girls in the world hadn't come to my office one day. I was chief probation officer by then, a big shot in a big office. I still can't fathom the courage it must have taken for those five poor, black teenagers to come knocking at this white man's door to tell their stories. I don't know what made them think I'd even listen, but I did listen, and what I heard was heart-breaking. Each of them had been recently released from Mt. Meigs. They showed me their bruises and scars as they told of being beaten with hoe handles and fan belts and brooms. Two of them had been sexually molested by men who worked there. They'd seen a pregnant girl beaten so badly she miscarried.

That day, Mt. Meigs became the crossroads of my life. I promised those girls and myself that I would find a way to change that place if I had to tear it down board by board. That decision put me at odds with just about everyone I knew as well as the people I worked for. It was the first step on a long path that eventually cost me my job and made me a pariah in the place where I'd grown up.

Before I tell you the rest, please bear with me while I tell you a little more about myself and about Montgomery, Alabama. You may already be thinking that all this sounds like something that happened long ago in a very strange place, but you are half wrong.

It wasn't really so long ago at all.

STORMS OF MY YOUTH. My mother and I stood on the front porch, watching the swirling, roaring mass as it wobbled our way. I can't describe it any better than that after all these years, but I'll never forget the fear in my belly.

I could not run away, because my feet were off the ground in an instant. My mother scooped me up and then, as soon as we were inside, pulled me down to the floor beside her. We both knelt and prayed, and we kept on praying until the monstrous thing had passed.

I had no real idea then what a tornado was, or what it was capable of doing, because I was only five years old. It wasn't until much later that I realized how lucky we were. The death toll in Montgomery alone on that day in February 1945 was twenty-six, with dozens more killed and injured as twisters blew apart homes and shops all across Alabama and Mississippi. The Associated Press report said the one that barreled through Montgomery actually picked up a freight train and ripped apart fifty box cars, scattering them "like match boxes."

This is how I remember my mother, cradling me against disaster. Goldie Magdalene Abbott was a woman of deep and abiding faith, which she had good reason to call upon daily. My father was drafted into the army during World War II when I was little more than a toddler, so Mom was left alone to care for me. It was a full-time job. I was what they called a sickly child, born with a raft of health problems that dogged me into adulthood. I had eczema so bad I was forced to wear gloves to keep from scratching through my skin. I also had asthma, and my breathing often became so labored that my mother had to call the doctor to rush over. Who wouldn't believe Dr. David Monsky was the answer to her prayers? He never failed to come to my rescue, even though he knew from experience there was no money to pay his bill.

We were poor enough to qualify for public housing, an apartment in a six- or eight-unit complex at 9 Pill Street. I didn't think it was a bad place at all. The Alabama River ran along the back of the property, and when you stepped out the door you almost always caught a whiff of fresh bread from the bakery two blocks down. It was enough to make a boy hungry, which was okay, because poor as we were we never lacked food — and my mother was a great cook. She baked fresh biscuits every morning so I could have them with my grits and eggs before going off to school. I'm sure she'd have baked another batch in the afternoon if I'd asked her to. She never stopped doting on me, although I somehow couldn't appreciate the luxury of being an only child and used to pray for a brother or sister. My mother had at least one miscarriage after I was born, but she never had another child. I remained her baby until the end of her life. I can still see her trying to comb my hair as I walked out the door to go to college.

Everything about my mother was sweetness and light, including her voice. She sang beautifully. Back in rural Alabama where she grew up, she once sang live on the radio accompanied on the guitar by her brother Elma, known as Buddy. She was the perfect counterpoint to my father, a man who was as blustery as that tornado and only slightly less intimidating.

Someone asked me not long ago what I think of when I picture my father. I didn't hesitate to speak the first word that came to mind: fear. He was a rough, tough guy who had to fight for everything he'd ever gotten, and he saw no reason to stop when he got home. He ruled not with an iron first but with a leather belt, which he laid into me more times than I care to think about. I wasn't always sure why, and he sure didn't feel obligated to explain himself. On the day he died, I was still saying "Yes, sir" and "No, sir"—and I was 60 years old at the time.

I have to give him this: Carl D. Abbott was, in many ways, a good father and husband, and he was always an honorable man. That was probably his most prized quality, and he did his best to instill it in me. He told me again and again that your word is your bond. He also told me to fight for what I believed in and stand my ground no matter who stood in my way. I've always done my best to live up to that.

Dad had an old-time Southern ethic that compelled him to provide for his family and to keep on working to improve our lot. He paid his bills and kept his word, always. As soon as he returned from the army, he went to Dr. Monsky and asked how much he owed for my care during the time he was gone. It took quite a while, but he paid every penny. That couldn't have been easy.

Dad worked for most of my childhood in one or another of Montgomery's meat-packing plants, where the pay was low and the work was brutal but steady. Like many poor kids from rural Alabama, he'd never set his sights very high. The one glimmer of promise in his early years had been football. He liked to boast that he was a professional athlete, a tenuous but not entirely unreasonable claim. He started off playing on his high school team back in Autaugaville, about twenty-five miles outside of Montgomery, where our family was something of a fixture. In fact, his father was once featured in the newspaper column *Ripley's Believe It or Not* as the first man in alphabetical order in the United States, a claim based on being the first name in the phone book in a town, county, and state that all started with "A." I still have the drawing that appeared with the column in a local paper showing Grandpa Clarence Daniel Abbott standing by a split-rail fence.

One day the high school coach from Prattville, about ten miles away, came to recruit my father. Dad was promised room, board, and maybe a little extra from time to time if he'd jump schools, so he did. It gave him a good story to tell for the rest of his life, but it wasn't incentive enough to keep him from quitting school and going off to work before he earned a high school diploma. It was common practice back then, but it almost always meant a life sentence at hard labor in a low-paying job. I know first-hand just how hard my father worked because he insisted I work at a meat plant every summer when I was in college. He said he wanted me to know the value of a dollar, but I'm sure he really wanted me to know the value of an education. I can't thank him enough for that.

Dad was just about the friendliest guy you can imagine, the sort of natural gabber who became instant friends with anyone he met. But in my father's world, you did not back away from a fight, and it didn't take much to get one started in a place where men were hot and angry and already feeling beat-up just from doing their jobs. I remember one summer I was part of a crew unloading dry salt pork bellies from a railroad car. We had the tops of our white coveralls down because it was so hot. Another guy and I just got into it—they didn't take kindly to a college kid coming in there and working for the summer. I'll never forget flailing around on the floor of that boxcar, salt everywhere, getting scraped up and beat up. I don't remember who won, and it doesn't matter. If you were going to work there, you were going to fight, and that's all there was to it.

There was no automation in those days either. A huge truck would rumble up to the loading dock, and men had to haul everything off by hand. You had to pick up the meat from the truck, carry it to the cooler, and wrestle it up on a hook. Some of those quarter sides of beef probably weighed 150 pounds.

At the plant where I worked, there was a door on the loading dock that had to be lifted by hand because it had a broken cable. The door must have weighed several hundred pounds. All the guys could open it easily, but I could barely budge it until the end of the summer, when I'd put on enough muscle. That's what working at the plant did to you.

Dad might have spent his whole life unloading rail cars if he hadn't had two exceptional talents: he was an absolute wizard with numbers, and he could talk like the devil. My father could multiply three-digit numbers in his head all day long and never make a mistake, and he could charm anyone into or out of just about anything. One day, somebody at the plant took notice and asked him to put down the beef and help with the books. He wound up pretty much running the place. This brought a dramatic change in our economic status.

I'd never really felt deprived, because my father always found a way to get what we needed, but now there was a little something extra to make life special. I made the Little League all-star team as a pitcher after he moved up to the office, and he bought me a Playmaker 22 leather glove. It probably cost eight or ten dollars, which doesn't sound like much now, but it was a very big moment for me. He bought me something else I treasured: my own shotgun. Every Southern boy learned to shoot from his father, and I was no exception.

I loved to go hunting with him. I remember many times going down to a little shack with my father and my cousins and some other male family members. We'd come back with thirty, forty, fifty squirrels. I've cleaned tons of squirrels, and I've eaten tons of squirrels. Lots of quail, too, and doves. It was a good feeling to have a shotgun in my hands, even though I was never a good shot. My dad was the best shot I've ever seen in my life. He didn't miss. I asked him how he got so good, and he said that when he was growing up you didn't dare miss, because you couldn't afford to waste the shells.

I LOVED HUNTING FOR another reason: it was beautiful in the Alabama woods, even in winter. (That was my favorite time to hunt because the snakes were in hibernation. I'm still petrified of snakes.) I thought everything about Alabama was beautiful, except maybe some of the old, run-down parts of Montgomery, but they were really no different from the old, run-down parts of any city. There was a stately Southern charm to Montgomery, with its old oak trees and wide streets and the Capitol with its towering columns—not that landscape or architectural details meant much to a kid. What I loved about growing up there most of all was hanging out with my pals. We had a club in junior high called the Hi-Y Club, and I was elected president. We'd climb in a big old truck and go on camping trips. I thought life was perfect, especially when we got to high school and we could climb in next to our girlfriends.

I kept pitching after Little League into Babe Ruth League and American Legion ball. I was pretty impressed with myself until I got to be seventeen or so. I had a dinky curve ball that never fooled anybody, so I was in real trouble when guys started teeing off on my fastball. I remember playing on a traveling team somewhere in the state, and the other team had a big catcher. I struck him out twice. When he came up late in the game, I reared back and threw as hard as I could, but he just pounded that thing. There were lights all around the center field fence, and I watched the ball sail up over those lights and out of sight. I never pitched again.

Looking back, I don't think there was a better place for a boy to grow up than Montgomery, at least as long as he was white—and I didn't know a single person who wasn't. If you are not from the South, and particularly from my generation, you may have picked up an image from movies or television of mean, white kids taunting and lording their superior status over black kids. None of my friends did that. We couldn't even if we had wanted to because we hardly ever saw black kids up close. There were no black children in any of the schools I attended. There were no black families in our neighborhood or in our church. Segregation was very much in force, and its effect was not just to keep blacks and whites apart but to make black people all but invisible to us. We lived in our world and they lived in theirs, which we had no reason to visit.

My father, however, wanted to be sure I learned everything he knew about black people. He shared his observations just about every night at dinner, almost all of them wrong and many downright nauseating when I think about them now. He believed every black person embodied the worst of every stereotype. And he never called them black, which hadn't come into use, or even Negro or colored, which were the polite terms back then. He always called them niggers. I can't say for sure that Dad was a member of the Ku Klux Klan because he never said so. But I'd have no trouble believing it, even though Dad tried not to sound mean-spirited and even made an occasional show of generosity by, say, tipping the black garbage collector. He often said he had no quarrel with black people "as long as they know their place and stop there."

Wherever their place was, it wasn't in our house. I never saw a black person under our roof until Dad got his promotion and we had money enough to hire a maid. I'd never heard my mother repeat the hateful things my father said about black people, but I'd never heard her argue with him either. I knew for sure she didn't feel the same way he did when I saw the respect she showed to our maid, Annie Mae. I really think Mom was as happy for the company as for the help. The two of them would have lunch together and chat as if they were at a ladies' tea party. One day my father came home unexpectedly and flew into a rage when he saw them. He could not stomach the idea of a black person and a white person sharing a meal anywhere, much less at his table.

My mother was no better-educated than my father, and she grew up in the same segregated culture, but somehow she didn't absorb any of that hate. She helped see to it that I didn't either. When we were alone, she told me the most remarkable thing I'd ever heard from a white person: she didn't think color made people better or worse than anyone else, and she thought everyone deserved to be treated decently. Maybe this seems unremarkable today, but it was incendiary back then, especially in the home of Carl D. Abbott.

We both knew better than to ever let him hear either of us repeat it.

THE STAR ON THE STAIRS. Like every city in the world, Montgomery has always boasted about its favorite sons and daughters.

Writer Zelda Fitzgerald was born there. Country music legend Hank Williams was born outside Birmingham, but his family moved to Montgomery when he was a teenager, and that's where his career started. Poet Sidney Lanier, born in Georgia, is considered an honorary native because he moved to Montgomery in the 1860s and wrote some of his most popular works there. Of course, not many people these days remember Sidney Lanier. The only reason I know about him is that I went to Sidney Lanier High School.

The one truly important historical figure most closely associated with Montgomery in my day was Jefferson Davis. Montgomery was the first capital of the Confederacy, and the Capitol is where Davis was sworn-in as its first and only president. This was still a huge deal when I was kid. A six-pointed brass star marks the spot between the columns on the top stair where Davis stood to take the oath of office on Feb. 18, 1861. It was a rite of passage for every boy I knew to march up those stairs and stand on that star. The Civil War probably seems like ancient history now to most Americans. Maybe it already seemed that way in the North by the time it was my turn to stand on that star. But in Alabama in the 1940s, white folks acted as though there was just a temporary lull in the fighting. I never met a Civil War veteran, although a few were still alive while I was growing up (I was 19 when the last Rebel died in 1958), but I remember talking to people whose grandfathers or great-grandfathers had told them how good it felt to shoot a Yankee. That didn't sound strange to me at all.

I was raised to be proud of the South and of the men who fought so valiantly to defend it. I never lost that pride, even as I grew to be appalled at the cause they championed. Even today, I still catch myself referring to the Confederates as "us." I certainly think of the Yankees as "them," and I'm never likely to change. It's too deeply ingrained.

Every year in Montgomery, the Blue-Gray Game kicked off the college football all-star season. The game featured players from Southern schools (the Gray) against players from the North (the Blue). Players from schools in the West were assigned to the Blue team. Only states that were part of the Confederacy qualified as Gray, even though the Southern players' jerseys were actually white. We looked at that game as nothing less than a resumption of war with the North. Everyone in town was in a frenzy. We celebrated like mad when the Grays won—and we were all miserable for weeks if they lost.

My pals and I didn't run across many Yankees at other times of the year, and we didn't care for them when we did. They thought they knew more than we did, and it was probably true because they went to better schools. We certainly weren't as sophisticated or worldly. Any time a Yankee came into the picture, we just saddled up the horses. It was us against them, and that's all there was to it.

This is the world and the mind-set I inherited when I was born into the most extraordinary time not only in Montgomery but in the entire South. Mine was the last generation of white privilege and dominance, and the first with a real opportunity to welcome change and even help it along. It was an opportunity most of the white people I grew up with didn't exactly embrace.

Montgomery had a reputation as one of the better cities for blacks in the entire South. At least, that was its reputation among white people. To an outsider, it probably seemed like blacks and whites got along just fine. It certainly seemed that way to most white people who lived there. And Montgomery probably really was better in a lot of ways than many other places. It did have a black middle class that was fairly well off economically, and you didn't often see the Klan marching down the street in full costume. Montgomery was mostly too polite for that sort of thing. Besides, it didn't need the Klan to enforce its racial divide because Montgomery was run by an entrenched, racist gentry that really believed it was beyond challenge. My friend Howard Mandell, who would come to play an important role in this story, explains it this way: "It wasn't just a city with a lot of racism, it was a city with a lot of blue-blood racism. Mobile was working class. Montgomery was blue blood. It was even more noxious for that reason."

I don't remember a whole lot of racial friction in my early years, but I may not be a reliable witness. Like most children, I was mostly interested in playing baseball and hanging out after school with my buddies. I had no idea that what's now called the Great Migration was going on, a vast exodus of blacks from the Old South to cities in the North where there were better jobs and no signs on restrooms warning "coloreds" to keep out.

I really don't remember exactly when the protests started, but a few controversies stand out in my mind after all these years. One involved the public pools at Oak Park, the big one for adults and a wading pool for children. Black people fought for the right to swim there for years. When they finally won a federal court ruling, the city shut down all of its parks and filled-in the Oak Park pools so they could never be used again by anyone. Most of the white people I knew thought that was perfectly reasonable. That was typical of the small-minded, mean-spirited adults I saw all around me as a child. I knew they were wrong, but I wasn't brave enough to say so — especially not to my father.

Of course, I do remember the Montgomery Bus Boycott of 1955 and 1956, which helped change the entire country. The house we moved to was just two blocks from the Cleveland Avenue route that Rosa Parks made famous. I rode that same bus route every day when I was in middle school. I took my seat up front in the whites-only section while black people had to sit in the back. They had to stand if it was too crowded, even if there were plenty of empty seats in the white section. It was actually illegal for blacks and whites to sit in the same row, so if the white section up front was full and another white passenger got on, every black person in the row closest to the front had to get up to make way. I knew instinctively that this was wrong, but it's easy not to think too hard about something you don't see. That's why the black people were sent to the back of the bus—so white people wouldn't have to see them. Black riders would climb the front steps to pay the driver, then get off the bus and walk around to enter through the back door. They had to exit from the rear, too. Sometimes they'd pay the driver but the bus would pull away before they could get on. Other times they barely made it.

I was in high school by the time all that came to an end. Everyone in the world must know the story of Rosa Parks, the black seamstress who refused to give up her seat to a white person. Actually, she wasn't the first black person to defy the rule.

Claudette Colvin, a fifteen-year-old high school girl, was arrested nine months before Parks when she refused to move to the back of a Montgomery bus. According to the news reports, Colvin was more than defiant; she was hysterical. Police dragged her off the bus as she flailed and screamed. The seat violation was legally no big deal, the equivalent of a speeding ticket, but Colvin was convicted of assaulting the policemen who arrested her. As a juvenile, she was placed on probation.

Colvin's case made national news, and even the *New York Times* carried a United Press report of her trial on March 19, 1955. Local civil rights leaders had been looking for a test case to challenge the city's segregated bus system, but they backed away from Colvin. They wanted a more sympathetic figure than an emotional teenager who was also pregnant and unmarried. This courageous and tough young woman, a year younger than I, was largely forgotten.

I have to admit, I didn't remember her name until I started compiling this book, but she and I will always be connected because our lives collided very hard with that of a man named William F. Thetford.

Thetford was Montgomery County's prosecuting attorney at the time of Colvin's arrest. Her lawyer pleaded with the court to spare his young client the stain of a conviction, but Thetford insisted she carry a criminal record. According to the wire service report, Thetford argued that the law must be obeyed regardless of whether it was right or wrong. The judge, not surprisingly, sided with Thetford.

As the struggle for civil rights brought increasing civil discord, Thetford insisted the courts mete out punishment regardless of the circumstances of the case or the unfairness of the law itself.

I have no doubt that he believed in the moral certainty of this position. He was a true Alabama blue blood. Born in Montgomery, he graduated from the Marion Military Institute in 1929 and earned his law degree at the University of Alabama in 1935. He practiced in Montgomery for a while, then became an FBI agent and went on the hunt for communists in New Jersey. He joined the navy during World War II as a lieutenant junior grade and rose to lieutenant commander while serving under heavy fire from Guam to the Philippines to Okinawa.

Thetford went back to private practice after the war before running for county solicitor in 1950. At age thirty-eight, he beat a man who'd held the job since before he was born. He proved time and again that he was a smart, thorough prosecutor with a solid grounding in the law and a command of court procedures. He was also racist to the core. I can say this without a doubt because I came to know him very well when he later became a judge. It is fitting that his lasting legacy was captured in the first sentence of his obituary in the Times as the man "who prosecuted the Rev. Dr. Martin Luther King Jr."

Dr. King was just becoming a familiar figure around town when I started high school. He came to Montgomery in 1954 after getting his doctorate at Boston University. He wasn't a legend then, just a dapper and determined young preacher who spoke out boldly and loudly against segregation. He quickly became the most forceful and compelling among a number of black ministers who were using their pulpits to champion the cause of racial equality. White people thought this was blasphemy, while white ministers openly preached segregation. I can't tell you how many times when I was growing up I heard people insist God didn't want the races to mix. They'd even tell you it was in the Bible, although they could never tell you exactly where.

Dr. King was easy for white racists to dismiss when he was

speaking to largely black audiences, but that changed dramatically after Parks was arrested on Dec. 1, 1955. Montgomery's black community, historically slow to organize, rallied to calls for a boycott of the bus system. Such boycotts had been held in other cities, but nothing on this scale. Black churches were instrumental not only in encouraging the movement but in keeping it going by organizing an elaborate ride-sharing and taxi system using parishioners' private cars. The boycott was noticed far beyond Montgomery, landing the city smack in the center of the civil rights movement. Dr. King, at the center of the boycott, suddenly found himself in the national spotlight for the first time.

He also became a target for all the anger and frustration of the white people who felt threatened by his message. Soon after Dr. King was elected to head the new Montgomery Improvement Association, his home was firebombed. Dr. King wasn't home, but his wife and baby were. He rushed back to find them safe, but he also found a throng of angry black supporters eager to confront a cordon of white police officers. As he would so famously do many times in the coming years, Dr. King made an impassioned plea for nonviolence and calmed the crowd.

None of this won him any sympathy from the white people who ran Montgomery. When they decided it was time to smash the boycott and its charismatic young leader, they turned to the obvious surrogate: Circuit Solicitor William Thetford. He was strangely reluctant to take up the cause. In fact, he actually argued against prosecuting Dr. King and other black leaders, but not because he had any sympathy for them. According to an article published in the Yale Law Review in 1989, Thetford complained that the law's penalties weren't harsh enough. He worried that small fines or even minor jail time would be shrugged off. He actually tried to persuade the privately owned bus line to sue Dr. King and the Montgomery Improvement Association in hopes of winning a jury award large enough to bankrupt the boycott's backers. But Thetford lost the argument, and he did his duty. He took the case to a grand jury and came back with nearly one hundred indictments naming Dr. King and other black ministers along with Rosa Parks—and, it seemed, anyone who had so much as said hello to any of them.

It all appears so clearly crazy now, this business of trying to put people in prison for refusing to ride a bus. But Thetford dusted off his law books and found an old anti-union statute that made it illegal to organize any activity designed to hurt a business without "just cause." The boycott was clearly aimed at hurting the bus line, and the cause of racial equality hardly qualified as just to Thetford and the white people he represented. All Thetford had to prove was that the boycott was well-organized, as it so obviously was, and that Dr. King and others were encouraging it. Dr. King was the first to be tried, and Thetford dispatched the case with skill and speed. The trial took place in March 1956, before a white judge with no jury. Dr King was convicted after just four days, but Thetford's fears turned out to be well-founded: the five-hundred-dollar fine didn't deter Dr. King or his supporters. The boycott not only continued but grew, along with Dr. King's stature. The trial drew national attention and helped bring his message of racial tolerance to a wider audience. It was a message that my father and his friends weren't ready to receive.

That year was one of the ugliest in all my time in Montgomery. White people tried every which way to break that boycott, probably as much to teach the black community a lesson as to save the bus line. They even dredged up a few Uncle Toms who tried to convince other black people that riding in back was just as good as riding up front, and way better than not riding at all. I never understood people like that. I mean, I understand why they acted that way—out of fear, or weakness, or simply because they were paid off—but I also saw the harm they did to good people who stood up for what they believed in and for what was right. I guess I just never understood how any black person could even think of helping the racists who beat them down and worked so hard to keep them there. The racists didn't quit even when the U.S. Supreme Court finally ruled in November that segregated seating on a public bus was unconstitutional: they started shooting at the newly integrated buses. Black riders were threatened. A black teenager was beaten when she got off at her stop.

The violence against black citizens became so bad it actually scared the people who ran Montgomery. They worried that even the magnetic Dr. King could not keep the black community from striking back with a vengeance. Once again, Thetford was called to action—this time, with a strange twist: he was expected to prosecute white people. You can read about this in Dr. King's own words in *A Testament of Hope: The Essential Writings and Speeches of Martin Luther King Jr.* According to Dr. King, the black community was surprised by the sudden arrest of seven white men in a series of bombings that had targeted black churches and homes, including the bombing of Dr. King's house. Five of the men were indicted, while charges against two were dropped. Dr. King was called as a witness in the trial of the first two defendants, Raymond D. York and Sonny Kyle Livingston.

Dr. King noted with irony that this was the same courtroom where he had been tried on the boycott charges and that the case was in the hands of the same prosecutor. He expected nothing more than a show trial that would end in acquittal. But his old nemesis surprised him. "Thetford fought as diligently for a conviction as he had fought for mine a year earlier," Dr. King wrote. "He had an excellent case."

The defense, playing on the sympathy of the white jury, cleverly put the blame on the victims. One of the lawyers insisted that "every white man, every white woman and every white child in the South . . . is looking to you to preserve our sacred traditions." Thetford countered by repeating his familiar theme: the law must be upheld no matter how you feel about it. "If you turn these men loose under the evidence that the state has presented, you say to the Ku Klux Klan 'if you bomb a Negro church or home, it's all right.' Then the next thing you know it will be your church and your house, because it's a sword that cuts both ways."

The jury took an hour and a half to return its verdict: not guilty on all charges. The courtroom packed with white people burst into applause. Dr. King was right in predicting the outcome, but he was mistaken if he thought Thetford's sympathies had changed. Three years later, they met again as adversaries in the same court. This time, Thetford was determined to win a felony conviction and send Dr. King to prison.

With his identity as a national leader firmly established, Dr. King moved to Atlanta in 1960 to begin his historic work at Ebenezer Baptist Church, but he was summoned back to Montgomery to deal with a complaint that he had under-reported income on his state tax returns some years earlier. Dr. King paid a $1,600 penalty under protest and returned to Atlanta. That would have ended most tax disputes, but Alabama's hard-line segregationist governor, John Patterson, saw an opportunity to permanently damage King's reputation. According to *The Journal of African-American History*, Patterson assigned the task to Thetford, who came up with an even more inventive charge than he had in the boycott case: perjury. Tax evasion wasn't a felony in Alabama, but perjury was. It didn't matter that no one in Alabama history had ever been charged with perjury in a tax case; the grand jury followed Thetford's instructions and indicted Dr. King on a charge that could have sent him to prison for up to five years. Once again, Thetford worked hard to win a conviction, but the case was so weak that the all-white jury saw through it, and Dr. King was acquitted. According to *The Journal of African-American History*, Thetford resisted pressure from the embarrassed governor to try Dr. King again on charges related to a second tax return: "When we tried him before, the jury didn't think we had a case and I don't think this case is any better."

That was the last joust between William F. Thetford and the Rev. Dr. Martin Luther King Jr. Even before his assassination, Dr. King eclipsed Jefferson Davis as the most important figure in Montgomery's history. He is also one of the most revered figures in America, the only person we honor with a national holiday solely in his name.

Three years after the King debacle, Patterson's successor made Thetford a county judge. It was the highest station he would achieve—and one that led him to play a pivotal role in my life.

TRYING TO MAKE A DIFFERENCE. Mom and I continued our whispered conversations about race and human dignity all through my high school and college years. I felt closer to her, emotionally and intellectually, than I ever did to my father. But I never showed any disrespect to him, and I never betrayed him behind his back. I looked up to my father, and I knew he loved me. He found his own ways to show it.

When I was fourteen or so, motor bikes were all the rage with my friends because that was the age when you could legally ride one. I told Dad I wanted one, and he blew his stack. He looked me in the eye and said, "You will never have a motor bike. They're dangerous. I don't want to hear another word about it." He could have left it at that, but he didn't. He promised that if I stayed in school, he'd buy me a car when I turned sixteen and he kept his word. My sixteenth-birthday present was a 1955 Ford. I don't remember if it was brand-new, but it must have been darn close to it.

My father succeeded despite his lack of education. He eventually left the packing plant and went to work selling life insurance. He was so persuasive he could have sold life insurance to a canary, but he knew he was still lucky to have escaped the loading dock, and he did not want to see me make the same mistake. He and my mother felt the same way about that. They never said, "if you go to college . . ." It was always "when you go to college . . ." I got the message, but I didn't really take it to heart. I never studied very hard or tried to excel at academics until years later, when I got to graduate school. I nearly flunked typing, of all things, in my senior year in high school, which would have kept me out of college. I was very lucky to squeak my way into Huntingdon College, a Methodist liberal arts school in Montgomery. Even then, I might have gotten sidetracked completely by the draft, but Dr. Monsky came to my rescue once again with a letter attesting to my lingering health problems. That got me classified 4F, allowing me the luxury of continuing to live at home until I finished college.

My father was as thankful to Dr. Monsky as I was, because he wanted me to focus on getting my college degree, but he never wanted anyone to think I was really a weakling. When I reached my twenties, he encouraged me to join him as a Mason and Shriner. After I completed the rigorous studies, I faced a daunting Shriner initiation that required candidates to be shocked "on the hot sands of Mecca," which was a cage charged with electricity. A doctor checked each of us to be sure we were healthy enough for the ordeal, and those who passed the exam were pinned with a red ribbon. My father stopped the ceremony as I was getting my ribbon. "Give him three ribbons," my father demanded. "He can take anything you can dish out." I took my shocks with pride, in myself and in my father.

I wasn't nearly as excited about school, drifting from semester to semester punctuated by grueling summers at the meat plant. Until senior year, I had no clear idea what I wanted to do when I graduated. I'd been dating Sharon Fulton, a classmate at Huntingdon, since the middle of junior year. Sharon was an air force brat who'd lived in many different places, including Peru. The only reason she was in Montgomery was that her father was stationed at Maxwell Air Force base outside town. She'd been born in Iowa, which made her think she was a Midwesterner, but my parents knew better. To them, she was a Yankee. Worse, she was a Catholic. Mom and Dad gritted their teeth when we announced our engagement during senior year.

Sharon and I graduated in May 1961, the month the Freedom Riders arrived and Montgomery exploded. I remember seeing them pull into the bus station a couple of blocks down from where I was standing. Everyone knew they were coming because there had already been trouble in Anniston and Birmingham. There was trouble everywhere they stopped across the South doing crazy things like walking into lunchrooms and sitting down, blacks and whites together. They were mostly college kids, mostly from the North, which meant they started with two strikes to most folks in our part of the country. I didn't argue when my friends called them outside agitators, but I probably didn't think too much about them one way or another. Mostly I was thinking about Sharon and getting married and what to do for a living. Looking back, I marvel at these kids. I wonder where they found the courage to get on a bus and risk their necks riding into such a forbidding and angry place?

Looking up the street, I saw the crowd—and I saw the clubs swing. I was too far away to see the blood, or hear the skulls crack. There wasn't a cop in sight. The whole city went berserk after that. Dr. King was speaking to the congregation at his former church that night when a crowd of men, women, and even children—all of them white—threw rocks through the windows. The city didn't quiet down until U.S. Attorney General Robert Kennedy sent in federal marshals and the governor imposed martial law. Thinking back, it's incredible: martial law is something you expect to hear about in other countries, not in an American city. Not in your hometown. It was only because of the federal authorities that any arrests were made in the attacks on the Freedom Riders. One of the men arrested was a friend of my father's and a known Klansman. I didn't see my father in the crowd, and he never said anything about it, but I've always wondered if he was there.

Sharon and I were married, barely a month after graduation. Now I had to find a job. My degree was in sociology, but that was almost by chance. I'd been called in to my counselor's office during senior year and told I had to pick a major. I had the most credits in sociology, so that was an easy choice. I hadn't really thought about how useful it might be until suddenly it was time to look for a job. I'd have taken just about anything, but there happened to be an opening at the county probation office. It sounded like a sociology degree might come in handy there, so I applied and I got the job. It paid $330 a month, gross, and I was thrilled to have it.

They Had No Voice

1

Learning the Limits of Social Theory

My job in 1961 in the Montgomery County juvenile justice system was to supervise kids who were on probation, and to place in custody at the detention center downtown the ones who'd violated their terms. The job turned out to be nearly impossible to do well. We had just four or five probation officers at the time, and a hundred children a month being shuffled through the youth court. Every kid assigned to me was supposed to come in each week with proof that he'd been going to school. If he wasn't in school, I needed to help him find a job and keep off the streets. But with eighty to a hundred children to keep track of, I quickly fell behind. A boy would come in, sit down across the desk, and I'd ask, "How are you? Fine? Everything good in school? Great. See you next week." And that was that.

I also realized quickly that social theory has its limitations when you're dealing with very angry people. On my first day at work, a boy I was trying to place in detention jumped me. Two days later, another boy's mother came after me with a knife. I backed away from her quickly, but I never backed away from even the toughest kids—and some of them were really tough. I remember many times rolling around the floor of the detention center with some 250-pound teenager who was trying to hurt me. Sometimes, a visit to a kid's house turned into a track meet when he'd see me and take off, and I'd have to go after him. One time, I was transporting a young man who managed to wriggle out the back window of my car when I stopped for gas. I chased him through a field that turned into a briar patch. I found myself in a world of hurt, thorns sticking me everywhere. I stopped cold, but the kid I was chasing just kept on boogying. Luckily, the state patrol caught up with him down the road.

Another time, a female probation officer, Janella Stephens, and I went looking for a girl who'd escaped from training school. When we got to the girl's home, I told Janella that I'd go in the back door while she waited in front in case the girl saw me and tried to run that way. I waited until my partner had time to get into position and then crashed through the back door of the apartment. I barged in on four guys playing poker. They didn't know if I was there to raid the game or arrest them. Money flew everywhere. I was as startled as they were, but I flashed my badge and they froze. I ordered them to stand against the wall as I edged toward the window. I looked out and saw Janella coming out of the apartment next door with the girl. That's when I realized I was in the wrong apartment. I told my "suspects" that I would let them go with a warning, and I got out of there quickly.

As tough as some could be, most of the children we dealt with were a far cry from the gangbangers who later came to terrorize so many cities. Assault was unusual and homicide almost (but not quite) unheard of. My wife kept a scrapbook of clippings from many of our cases, and the headlines from the early days seem almost quaint nowadays:

"Egg-Throwing Youths Are Sought by Police," "Purse Snatching Believed Ended by Boys' Arrest," "Young Billfold Thieves Caught," or "Vandals 'Open' 38 Fire Hydrants," to give a few examples.

These were children who might be steered back onto an honest path if someone reached them in time. You've heard it said that the most likely time to solve a murder is within forty-eight hours of the crime? Well, the time to get a young offender's attention is within twenty-four to forty-eight hours of his first arrest. That's when they're scared, when they want desperately to find a way out of the mess they're in. If I could show them there was a way, they might just take it. But when too much time went by, they became resentful—and then downright defiant. You could hear it in their voices. You could see it in the swagger when they walked.

I never got into serious trouble as a kid, probably because I was too afraid of what my father would do, but also because I kept busy. When I wasn't playing baseball I was playing basketball, or I was coaching younger children at the YMCA. I didn't hang out with a tough crowd, but we weren't immune to making a little mischief now and then. One time in high school, we all piled into my Ford and went to a drive-in movie to flirt with girls and drink beer. Back then, nobody thought much one way or the other about drinking and driving, even if technically we were too young to drink and barely old enough to drive. On the way home, we realized the floor of the car was covered with empty beer cans. I had to get rid of them before I got home, so we started tossing them out the window.

We didn't get far before I saw flashing lights in the mirror. I think the cop might have let us go with a warning if one of my pals hadn't started making wisecracks, which the cop didn't find very funny. He called the paddy wagon and had us all taken away. It was the first and only time I've ever been locked in a cell. Worse than that, I had to call my father to come and get me out. I was prepared for a beating, or at least to have him take away my car, but all I got was a stern lecture and a warning not to do that again. Then he called his friend the chief of police and asked him to take care of things. And that was the end of it. Whatever record

I'd compiled in my one-night career as a dangerous criminal was permanently erased.

Right or wrong, that's how things were done in those days. By the time I became a probation officer, the system had become a bit more formal, if not necessarily more sophisticated. A newspaper picture from July 1962 shows me standing sternly in front of three teens who'd been caught after wrecking a car they stole. They'd been placed on probation plus sentenced to a week in detention, but that wasn't the toughest part. When the boys were caught, each proudly sported a "ducktail" haircut, which high school principals and other serious adults considered a sure symbol of juvenile delinquency. The judge ordered their heads shaved. In the newspaper photo, the boys are all facing me, and the backs of their heads are shining at the camera lens as an object lesson to other budding thieves.

The judge was Richard P. Emmet, who presided over our family and juvenile court. He was a young man from an old Montgomery family who was determined to make a big impression. Barely thirty, he was active in the Jaycees and just about every other civic group in town. He was also my boss, because the chief probation officer reported to the judge, but I rarely dealt with him directly. I reported to the chief probation officer, Tom Esslinger, a good guy who treated me fairly and wasn't afraid to raise a fuss with our elected officials about the county's inadequate and outdated detention facilities—not that it did much good.

Our short-term holding facility was at the county courthouse downtown, on the third floor behind a set of double-locked steel doors. Any sentence of more than an hour there should have been considered cruel and unusual punishment. The place consisted of little more than bare walls and floors. The kids slept in four dorm rooms, on mattresses laid side-by-side on the floor. Each room was designed to hold four children but usually held at least twice that many. There were also two larger recreation rooms—a somewhat humorous term, considering there was little possibility of recreation except for an old TV, a handful of books, and a rickety Ping-Pong table. There was no counseling, no teaching, no training.

With just a handful of probation officers, no one was on duty at the detention center most of the day except a matron, so the children couldn't be let out of their rooms. Except for their two hours of communal time each day, there was nothing for any of them to do but sit on their mattresses and stare at each other. Space was even tighter because we had to keep blacks and whites on separate sides of the facility. And with no air conditioning, the whole place was stifling hot in summer. Yet we kept these young people in detention for up to a month, sometimes more if there was no room at the long-term facilities out of town. It was hardly surprising that some of them became so desperate they'd smash through the steel window mesh and try to climb down on bed sheets.

CHILDREN FACING LONGER SENTENCES were committed to what the state called "training schools." White kids went to separate facilities for boys and girls near Birmingham. Both were good places, and not just for Alabama. They were clean and well-equipped, with solid counseling and vocational programs. Black boys and girls all went to Mt. Meigs.

As feisty as some kids were when they were first arrested, the fight had pretty much drained out of them by the time they were ready to be transported to reform school. The kids headed for Mt. Meigs were especially quiet along the way. We made the half-hour trip in county cars, mostly four-door Chevrolets. You could put a kid in the back seat and not worry too much that he'd jump out, because the inside door handles were removed and the windows were rigged to roll down just enough for ventilation. If I had a particularly difficult customer back there, I clamped my handcuffs on him just to be extra safe. I still have them: Chief of Police brand, model 8579, double-lock steel.

The trick with handcuffs is never to clamp them too close to the hand. You have to keep them above the little bones in the wrist because that's what keeps them from slipping off. If you do that, you don't have to make them uncomfortably tight. I figured these kids were uncomfortable enough just thinking about where they were going.

Outside of town, I'd head east on the Atlanta Highway, a flat, four-lane, divided road that sliced through farms and cotton fields dotted with shacks that probably had been standing at least since the Civil War. Mt. Meigs fit in perfectly with its surroundings. There was nothing to announce its presence: no gate, no fence, no security—nothing to stop a kid from just walking away, except fear. Every building on the grounds looked exactly like those farm shacks along the way, dilapidated and beaten down by the years. I don't remember the first boy I took there, but I will never forget what I saw as I walked with him from the car to the tumbledown administration building: an army of children trudging through the fields. The image of an army is fixed in my mind because when I got close, I could see they were wearing surplus fatigues, almost all of them too big. The littlest ones tripped over the legs of their too-long pants as they hacked at the ground with shovels and hoes. Apparently the state could not afford enough surplus shoes, because many of the children were barefoot, whether picking crops, slopping hogs, or digging trenches. They looked like the ghosts of some defeated army that had been put to work on an antebellum plantation and forgotten.

Knowing Alabama and the South as I did, I was hardly surprised that a school for black children would be rundown and poorly equipped. But the image of those barefoot children stayed with me. Even without knowing the true horror of the place, I knew this: time served at Mt. Meigs was not likely to make any child a better citizen, much less a better person.

I wasn't the first to be shocked by what I saw at Mt. Meigs, which over the years had been the subject of continuing complaints—not about the way the children were treated, but about the deteriorating condition of the facilities. In response to a newspaper series that focused on the school's ramshackle appearance, the legislature appointed a special committee in the spring of 1963 to investigate the "outmoded buildings, overcrowded and unsanitary conditions and generally disgraceful surroundings." A resolution passed by both houses noted a "state of affairs and conditions existing to shock the conscience of all loyal Alabamians." Yet the state was apparently able to absorb this shock with little difficulty. Hundreds of thousands of dollars were appropriated for improvements at the school over the next several years—but where most of the money went is a mystery. Very little of importance at Mt. Meigs was rebuilt or fixed or even cleaned up; clearly, there was no sense of urgency regarding the children. The committee's final report noted that "the children looked fairly well clothed and quite well fed and seemed healthy. The relationship between the children and the staff seemed excellent."

How CAN IT BE that I was haunted by my vision of those haggard boys and girls in sagging fatigues, while a committee of legislators and judges could view those very same children toiling in those same fields and conclude that all was well? Welcome to the South of the 1960s. In many ways, it was not so different from the South of the 1860s, when white slave owners looked out across their fields and imagined a legion of happy darkies who were thankful to serve their "massas."

One of the clippings I kept illustrates perfectly the prevailing sentiment toward blacks in general and teenagers in particular. The one-column story from the *Montgomery Advertiser* is headlined, "White Men Get Fines in Negro Beating." The victim was a sixteen-year-old employee at a local stockyard who had failed to move out of the way quickly enough when a white man tried to get around him on a catwalk. The youth was forced into a car at gunpoint and driven to an empty storage building, where he was beaten by five men. Police who arrived at the hospital noted he was "beat up pretty bad." Two men were arrested and convicted, but they were spared jail time. Instead, they were fined one hundred dollars. Even at that, the judge apparently felt the need to explain such a tough sentence by calling the beating an aggravated case and noting the region's "race tension," which was code for, "We have to look like we're doing something or the Negroes will riot."

I was required to routinely lock up children for crimes as petty as shoplifting a pair of shoes or vandalizing a newspaper rack, but these grown men who viciously beat a black teenager never saw the inside of a jail cell. What message did that send? I saw many examples of law enforcement's racist mentality in my years as a probation officer. I rode with Montgomery police from time to time and saw them steal at will whenever they entered a black person's home. Many times I saw officers sweep up money from a card game and put it in their pockets. I remember once when police were called to the home of a black man and woman who weren't married. A cop told them they were breaking the law by living together and they had to get married on the spot or he'd arrest them. He charged them ten dollars to perform a phony marriage ceremony, which consisted of mumbling nonsense while he stared into his ticket book. I'm sure the couple knew it was a con job, but what choice did they have? Black people understood from such experiences that they would not get a fair shake from the police or the courts, regardless of whether they were victims or the accused.

In fact, black people could not get a fair shake anywhere in Alabama as long as it was run by racists like Governor John Patterson, who trounced his only slightly more moderate opponent in the 1958 election. That opponent was a farm boy-turned-lawyer named George Wallace, who swore after his defeat that he would never be "out-segged" again. Wallace made good on his vow when he ran for governor a second time in 1962, whooping and posturing against any federal interference in his state's "right" to keep black people in poverty and subservience. He won by a landslide.

On January 14, 1963, Wallace literally followed in the footsteps of Jefferson Davis to take the oath of office on the Capitol steps. As he addressed the crowd, he paid tribute to Davis as well as to Confederate General Robert E. Lee, calling Alabama "the very heart of the Great Anglo-Saxon Southland" and promising to defend white supremacy against all enemies: "In the name of the greatest people that have ever trod this earth, I draw the line in the dust and toss the gauntlet before the feet of tyranny, and I say: segregation today, segregation tomorrow, segregation forever."

It was yet another message of despair rather than hope for the young black people of our state. Working with youthful offenders, I could see firsthand the effects of hostility and unfairness, especially for the children committed to Mt. Meigs.

DESPITE MY FRUSTRATIONS, I enjoyed my job. I cared about my work, and I liked working with other people who cared about their work. I got along well with my colleagues. More important, I respected them. I particularly came to respect and like Vernon Baker, one of the few black probation officers in the department. I liked Vernon so much that Sharon and I invited him and his wife to our home for dinner, with predictable fallout: my dad went on a rant, and the neighbors stopped talking to us for a while.

The best thing about my job was that once in a while, I really did believe we helped a kid. Maybe we didn't help too often, and maybe we didn't help enough, but it felt good just to try. The low pay didn't even bother me, in part because Sharon was the most frugal person I'd ever met. She made just about everything she needed around the house. We didn't even feel a pinch when our first child, Courtland David—the fourth generation of C. D. Abbotts—was born in 1962. Two more children, Kimberly Ann and Andrew Scott, followed in the next two years. (I told you my wife was Catholic!) Sharon made clothing for all the children.

My perseverance paid off much more quickly than I expected. I'd been on the job a little over two years when my boss, Tom Esslinger, decided to quit and go to graduate school. Although I wanted his job, I figured I had little hope because I was one of the youngest and least-experienced of the officers working under him. The ambitious Judge Emmet got his own promotion about that time when he was appointed to fill a vacancy on the circuit court. One of his last official acts before moving on was to appoint me to take Tom's place. At twenty-three, I became the youngest chief probation officer in Alabama and undoubtedly the most eager. I had a head full of ideas and unlimited confidence in my ability to make them work.

I got my chance under the man Governor George Wallace picked as Judge Emmet's successor: the Honorable William F. Thetford.

2

Seeking Justice

I didn't wait long to make big changes in the probation office. Early on, I moved my staff out of the courthouse and into the housing projects.

We matched one case file after another to a map of Montgomery and pinpointed where the most troubled children lived. Then I persuaded the housing authority to let us use vacant apartments as offices for probation officers, right in the kids' backyard. The idea wasn't just to keep a closer eye on them—although that certainly didn't hurt—but to be there when a child needed help. Even a few minutes can make a world of difference to children whose mothers would be out prostituting all day and whose fathers were either gone or drunk. They'd come home to an empty house, or a beating. Now we could counsel them on the spot instead of waiting for them to get into trouble. It worked. There was a significant decrease in juvenile crime in those neighborhoods over the next several years.

Not only was I promoted to chief probation officer, I got a second job as the youth court's judicial referee. It didn't bring me any additional pay, but it was a significant step up in responsibility. As referee, I held detention hearings and determined which children should be released within twenty-four hours of arrest and which would be held until their court dates. I took this responsibility seriously, studying each case and weighing the facts. My lack of legal training wasn't an issue. In fact, I was more qualified than many judges around the state. Most rural counties didn't even have youth courts. They relied on the local probate judge, who wasn't necessarily a lawyer and wasn't even required to have a high school diploma. In a lot of places, he was the guy who also ran the grocery store or the gas station.

The justification for this insanity was that juvenile delinquency wasn't a crime, it was a civil infraction. Sort of like a parking ticket, but with one big difference: kids who were declared delinquent were locked up, and they could stay locked up for a year without ever seeing a lawyer or having a trial. Sometimes they were locked up for doing nothing more than annoying the wrong adults, including their parents. People could come into court and say, "I can't handle this kid. He's out of control." That didn't mean the child had done anything remotely criminal. Maybe he just stayed out late night after night, or ran away from home. With girls especially, even the suspicion of sexual activity could be enough to send parents running to court. All they had to do was declare that the child was incorrigible (whatever that meant) and if the judge was convinced—bingo: the kid was sent to reform school by a guy wearing a Sunoco hat.

Thetford, at least, was a real judge and an educated man. Better still, he seemed to like me. He was also a Mason and Shriner, so perhaps he felt a kinship of sorts. We never had casual conversations or developed anything like a friendship, but it was his idea to make me a referee, and he also routinely backed my administrative and personnel decisions. Although he was in his fifties, he still appeared lean and vigorous, with a full head of hair combed in a modest pompadour. He spoke directly but softly, and he chain-smoked Picayune cigarettes ("Pride of New Orleans"). I might have grown to like the man if he hadn't shown his ugly side early on.

Thetford was always courteous to the parents of white children who appeared before him, but he refused to acknowledge the parents of black children. If they tried to speak to him, he simply ignored them—and he expected all of us to act the same way. One day, Thetford called the entire probation staff into his chambers and announced that anyone who referred to a "nigger" in his courtroom as "Mr." or "Mrs." would be fired. He didn't elaborate and never explained what set him off. He also didn't hesitate to make his pronouncement in the presence of several black employees. None of us challenged him, because there was clearly no chance of changing his mind.

Suddenly we were all on notice that a lack of common courtesy toward black people was a condition of employment. I wasn't sure Thetford could follow through on his threat, because I was a civil service employee with at least theoretical protection from arbitrary dismissal, but I didn't want to test that protection. I'd like to say I knew Thetford would get his comeuppance soon enough because the days of white supremacy were obviously numbered, but none of us could see the signs that are so clear in hindsight.

Montgomery remained a battleground in the civil rights movement throughout my years as chief probation officer. Long after Dr. King moved to Atlanta, he came back time and again to lead prayers and protests. I remember watching through a courthouse window as he marched down Dexter Avenue.

Everyone knows about the 1965 march from Selma that ended as quickly as it began in a violent clash with state police at the Edmund Pettus Bridge. Two marches followed. On the third try and after five days, the marchers completed the fifty-plus-mile hike to Montgomery. It took nearly four thousand federal troops and National Guardsmen to protect them along the way and to keep peace in Montgomery once they arrived. The Klan did everything it could to make their job harder: I still have one of their leaflets warning that black men were coming to town to have sex with white girls. When it became clear that nobody was going to stop the marchers from entering the city, white folks pretty much abandoned the place for the day. I probably wasn't smart enough to go with them. When Dr. King addressed a crowd of twenty-five thousand from the same Capitol steps where Jefferson Davis took the oath of office, I was standing on the first step. King said:

> Now it is not an accident that one of the great marches of American history should terminate in Montgomery, Alabama. Just ten years ago, in this very city, a new philosophy was born of the Negro struggle. Montgomery was the first city in the South in which the entire Negro community united and squarely faced its age-old oppressors. Out of this struggle . . . a new idea, more powerful than guns or clubs was born. Negroes took it and carried it across the South in epic battles that electrified the nation and the world.

It's impossible to read these words today and not feel stirred, but I knew plenty of people back then who still considered Dr. King and his followers troublemakers—and others who seemed to truly believe that the whole civil rights movement would melt away if only they held their ground. The commitment of the federal government—the Yankee government—did not impress or persuade people like my father and Judge Thetford. To them, the Civil Rights Act of 1964, the Voting Rights Act of 1965, and a growing series of federal court rulings were mere insults.

Still, I didn't argue with Judge Thetford about matters of race any more than I argued with my father. I had more than job security at stake in not wanting to antagonize him: Thetford was a politician with important allies who might help us get the money we needed to do a better job. Events were making that an urgent necessity. The strain on our facilities had grown since I started working in the probation office, and the situation continued to deteriorate as the raucous 1960s finally intruded on quiet old Montgomery. More children were being charged with serious and even violent crimes, as headlines about flying eggs gave way to headlines about flying bullets: "Two Youths Shot in Rioting After Ball Game," "Boy Charged in Stabbings," and "Three Charged in Beatings" were typical.

These crimes also had more-serious consequences, as the *Montgomery Advertiser* reported one day:

> Boy Succumbs Following Fight
>   A 13-year-old Montgomery Negro died after a fight at the
> May Street Tavern in Montgomery late Monday morning.

The kids committing serious offenses were younger too, like the eleven-year-old who set fire to a church because he wanted to see the fire trucks and crowds. What do you do with a kid like that? We had no place for him except the detention center, which was already crowded with older, tougher kids.

Outrages like this started drawing the attention of the press and community groups. A county grand jury zeroed in on the detention center in a July 1965 report, calling it inadequate. The *Montgomery Advertiser* followed up with a series of articles highlighting the shortage of probation officers and lack of options for housing and rehabilitating offenders. The National Council on Crime and Delinquency warned that the situation in our detention center was so dire that "someone could get killed in those crowded rooms." The group's expert recommended expanding our probation staff from five to twenty-four. A new detention center and vastly expanded staff and resources were essential, the council concluded.

The state's facilities were overflowing just like ours, but they found an easy solution: whenever they ran out of room, they just refused to take more children. There wasn't much I could do about that except complain, but I complained loudly and publicly. The day I took the job as chief probation officer, I decided that I would not defend a system that was inadequate, outdated, and dangerous. Instead, I spoke out every chance I got.

Judge Thetford gave me a boost around this time by recommending that the county pay my way through graduate school. It was an incredible opportunity. Montgomery agreed to continue paying my salary for nine months while also paying tuition plus room and board for me and my family as I attended Florida State University in Tallahassee. In return, I agreed to continue in my job for at least five years after finishing school. I left at the end of summer in 1965 and returned the following May, having completed the coursework I'd need for a master's degree in criminology and corrections. I was eager to put my new knowledge to use while I wrote my thesis and prepared to defend it, but I found my energy again diverted by the worsening crisis in our detention facility.

At the center of this latest controversy was a man who would come to play as large a role in my life as Judge Thetford, a brilliant and gutsy thirty-four-year-old attorney named Ira De Ment. Like Thetford, De Ment was from an old Alabama family, attended Marion Military Institute, got his law degree from the University of Alabama, and joined the Masons and Shriners. He also served with distinction in the military, earning a Distinguished Service Medal (one step above the Silver Star) and serving as a judge advocate general before ultimately retiring as a major general in the U.S. Air Force Reserve. Of course, back then he was a mere lieutenant colonel, but I'd have easily believed he was chairman of the Joint Chiefs of Staff, judging by his upright military bearing and precisely clipped speech. I could also have taken him for a professor, with his horn-rimmed glasses and elegant language. By any measure, he was an impressive man.

I got my first close-up look at him soon after my return to Montgomery, when he came to the defense of a sixteen-year-old girl who'd violated probation by running away to get married. One of my officers picked her up and brought her to the detention center while we waited to transfer her to the Girls' Training School in Chalkville. More than a month later, we were still waiting, and so was she. The state insisted the school was full, and we couldn't let her go without taking a chance that she'd run away again.

In arguing for her release, De Ment challenged the constitutionality of the entire family court system, which gave the judge near-complete authority to order a child held as a delinquent. He also laid out all the weaknesses and inadequacies of our aging detention center. It was a compelling argument against locking up any child in such a place. Unfortunately, De Ment was forced to make the argument before Judge Thetford, who refused to even hold a hearing on the girl's case. "I deplore the conditions of the present juvenile detention facility but it is the only facility available," Thetford said. De Ment didn't give up, however, and the Alabama Court of Appeals ordered Thetford to give the girl her day in court. Finally, she was released on bond—and this time, she didn't run away.

I was the first witness, and I was thrilled by the opportunity. I told the truth, which could only help the girl and all the others to follow: our detention center was as bad as De Ment claimed, and maybe worse. I testified that we offered no psychological testing, no outdoor recreation, no religious services, and no schooling, and that the children in our care never saw a doctor unless they were very sick. When asked if we were upholding our legal obligations to the children in our custody, I told the truth again: no, we were not. The girl's testimony was even more damning than mine. She described being held locked in a room with no windows and no lights. She was told the light was broken and no repairman was available on weekends. She stayed in the dark for three days. It was seven more days before she was transferred to a room with windows. She saw daylight only once during her confinement, when she was taken to a doctor.

De Ment ended with a dramatic appeal for a new detention center as well as freedom for his client. If Thetford was moved by any of this, he hid it well. The judge concluded the hearing by placing the girl back in my custody and ordering me to try again to find a place for her at the training school. We both knew that a bed had already opened up, so I had no choice but to follow orders and send her away.

IRA DE MENT LOST, but he made a deep impression on me and on the public. The case focused new attention on the problems in our system and brought added momentum to the push for a new detention center. I was determined to keep the momentum going. I had been speaking to civic groups ever since starting the job, and most often my topic was the need for a new center. Now it was my only topic, and I was determined to speak everywhere I could wangle an invitation: the Kiwanis Club, the Catoma School PTO, the Dalraida Baptist Church, the Queen of Mercy PTO, the Ladies Group of the Trinity Presbyterian Church. Everywhere I went, I issued an invitation to come see just how awful things were. Whenever anyone hesitated, I reminded them that they owned the detention center, because it was supported by their tax dollars. I just worked there.

More often than not, at least some in the group accepted my invitation to tour *their* detention center. I spoke to hundreds of groups, so that turned out to be a lot of people—most were shocked by what they experienced. I think the smell got to them more than anything. I always moved the children out of the way first to protect their privacy, but the smell of all those people living side-by-side in those small quarters lingered in the stale air. The sounds were almost as disturbing. Every voice echoed, every door clanked in this hollow chamber with no furniture and concrete walls. I'd ask each group: is this the sort of place where you'd want your child to spend even a few hours? Before escorting them out, I'd remind everyone once again: You own this place. Are you proud of it? If not, let's do something about it. I think nearly everyone left determined to do exactly that. Many responded by calling or writing to local officials or the press, or attending public meetings.

The county finally began to respond by approving various studies and considering and rejecting different proposals. Meanwhile, the news kept getting worse. In October 1966, three girls smashed through the detention center screening and leaped forty feet to the ground. Miraculously, they weren't seriously injured. Almost immediately after that, the county finally coughed up money to hire extra supervisors. The following August, two teenage boys in our care were raped by adult inmates in the county jail. They should never have been in there, but we had no room for them in the detention center. Soon after that, the county finally agreed to put a $750,000 bond issue for a new detention center to a countywide vote in December 1967.

I kept up my hectic speaking schedule as the vote neared. A week before, Ira De Ment appeared in court again, this time seeking the release of ten boys we were holding in detention as they waited and waited to be accepted by Mt. Meigs. Again, I was thankful that he helped keep the spotlight on the problem. Both local newspapers also jumped in to help by endorsing the bond proposal. Just to make sure voters got the message, I took out a paid advertisement adding my own endorsement.

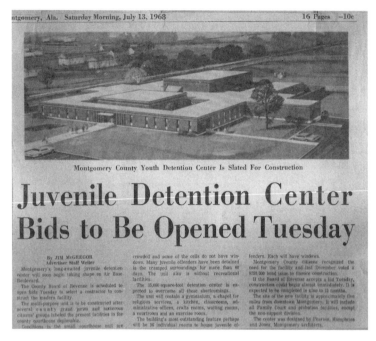

Montgomery County Youth Detention Center Is Slated For Construction

Juvenile Detention Center Bids to Be Opened Tuesday

By JIM McGREGOR
Advertiser Staff Writer

Montgomery's long-awaited juvenile detention center will soon begin taking shape on Air Base Boulevard.

The County Board of Revenue is scheduled to open bids Tuesday to select a contractor to construct the modern facility.

The multi-purpose unit is to be constructed after several county grand juries and numerous citizens' groups labeled the present facilities in the county courthouse deplorable.

Conditions in the small courthouse unit are crowded and some of the cells do not have windows. Many juvenile offenders have been detained in the cramped surroundings for more than 60 days. The unit also is without recreational facilities.

The 35,000-square-foot detention center is expected to overcome all these shortcomings.

The unit will contain a gymnasium, a chapel for religious services, a kitchen, classrooms, administrative offices, crafts rooms, waiting rooms, a courtroom and an exercise room.

The building's most outstanding feature perhaps will be 36 individual rooms to house juvenile offenders. Each will have windows.

Montgomery County citizens recognized the need for the facility and last December voted a $750,000 bond issue to finance construction.

If the Board of Revenue accepts a bid Tuesday, construction could begin almost immediately. It is expected to be completed in nine to 11 months.

The site of the new facility is approximately five miles from downtown Montgomery. It will include all Family Court and probation facilities, except the non-support division.

The center was designed by Pearson, Humphries and Jones, Montgomery architects.

I'm still a little shocked at how handily we won. The bonds passed by an eight-to-one ratio, nothing short of miraculous in a place as conservative as Montgomery. I felt truly proud to live in a community willing to sacrifice for the kids so many people just don't care about. In the months that followed, I traveled around the country touring juvenile detention facilities with the architects hired to design our new center. I wanted to find the best and make sure ours turned out to be better. There's probably a more elegant way of putting it, but all this made me feel really great. I wasn't yet thirty years old, and I'd proven that I could help shape public opinion about a vital issue. People all over the city knew my name, the press quoted me, my co-workers respected me. I was well on my way to earning an advanced degree from a major university, and I was earning a pretty good living—good enough to buy a brand-new house. And as hard as I worked for

other children, I always made time for my own: I was probably
the only male PTA president in Alabama.

There was only one problem in my professional life that I'd
failed to solve, but it was the one that troubled me most: Mt. Meigs.

As BUSY AS I was running the department and planning for the
new detention center, I never stepped completely away from being
a working probation officer. I couldn't ask my already overbur-
dened staff to take on more cases, so I continued to track kids,
visit their homes, and ferry them to and from reform school. That
meant dozens of visits to Mt. Meigs each year. I never got past the
administration building, never saw the inside of the dormitories
or classrooms, but I got a vivid picture of those places from a story
in the *Montgomery Advertiser* by the city editor, Colin MacGuire,
on July 11, 1967. The story discussed and the photo spread showed
pools of raw sewage around the dorms, rotting rafters and sagging
floors in the dining hall, and a heating system that consisted of
two pot-bellied stoves. The story reported that state money was
on the way to fix at least some of these problems—but money
was always on the way to Mt. Meigs. It just never seemed to get
there, or do much good even if it did arrive.

The *Advertiser's* report was clearly sympathetic to the school's
long-time superintendent, E. B. Holloway. I was skeptical about
his sincerity because I'd encountered him many times at the
school and at the courthouse. He was an older, weather-beaten
black man who looked like what he really was—a farmer, not a
teacher or administrator. His professional credentials were about
on par with those gas-station judges: he claimed to have studied
agriculture at the Tuskegee Institute, but he never got a college
degree. He worked for fifteen years as a farm agent before going
to Mt. Meigs in 1947 to run the farming program. Somehow, he
was elevated to the head job in 1952, even though the state statute

governing Mt. Meigs required the school's superintendent to have "training and experience in social case work and institutional management . . ."

I could see why Holloway was well-liked by the politicians who protected him. He had the quality they prized most highly among black people: he never argued with a white man. He was a true Uncle Tom who shuffled and smiled like a character from an old movie, except he was hardly benign.

When the reporter asked about the sorry state of his facility, Holloway complained about the lack of state support—but also boasted about how clever and enterprising he'd been in keeping the place afloat with such limited resources. For years, the State of Alabama had justified short-changing Mt. Meigs at budget time by claiming that farming made the school nearly self-supporting. Holloway bragged that cotton and cucumbers brought in cash, while hogs provided all the fresh meat a growing child needed. Better yet, these children were said to be learning real job skills. Who could argue with any of it?

Certainly few white people in Alabama expected black delinquents to aim for anything higher than the life of a farmhand. In fact, most white folks probably thought these children should be downright thankful for being treated so well. I knew better because of what I'd seen. These children who scraped at the dirt with home-made hoes weren't learning job skills; they were working someone else's fields, just as their grandparents and great-grandparents had done under that same, broiling Alabama sun. I also knew what they weren't learning: reading, writing, or even simple math. It was obvious that children who spent their days in the fields weren't spending enough time in the classroom. Meanwhile, white children at other reform schools were getting a real education—and they weren't picking cotton.

None of this was supposed to be my concern, or anyone's

concern except for Holloway and the board of trustees he reported to. It was no accident that Holloway and all the others who lived or worked at Mt. Meigs were black and the members of the board of trustees, who were appointed by the governor, were all white. The board included some of the most prominent people in town; almost all were major landowners whose farms ringed the countryside around Mt. Meigs. Years later, I learned the real reason these trustees were so supportive of Holloway: he provided them with an endless supply of free, child labor. Whenever the trustees needed their fields plowed, or their crops picked, or their lawns mowed, they'd send their trucks over to Mt. Meigs and cart off as many children as they could carry. These boys and girls became slaves in the most literal sense of the very people who were supposed to see that they were educated and rehabilitated.

This, in turn, explains why those same prominent citizens turned their backs while so many of the children were subjected to unspeakable horrors. Years later, a handful of men whose lives were ruined by their childhood experiences at Mt. Meigs finally got a chance to testify in court. The brutality they described was so widespread, so much a part of the daily routine, that it could not have been missed by anyone who made an earnest attempt to inquire about the children's welfare.

As for those hogs, they did provide an abundance of meat, but not for the children, who were forced to raise and butcher the animals only to stand by and watch the trustees and their pals pick over the carcasses. Every decent cut was taken away to be sold or eaten by the trustees and their families, or their dogs. Only the scraps and snouts and bones were left to be boiled into soup to feed the children.

Nobody tried to hide any of this because they didn't have to. Mt. Meigs was as invisible to the white people of Montgomery as any other place inhabited by black people. In fact, Mt. Meigs had become invisible to most black people too. Like our long-neglected county detention center, it was a place where most parents wanted to believe their own children could never end up. Simply put, nobody saw what was happening at Mt. Meigs because nobody wanted to. So this horrific outrage—the enslavement of children—went on year after year just a few miles from the place where thousands risked their lives for the right to ride in the front of a bus.

I might have turned away from Mt. Meigs just as so many others did if I had had a choice, but I didn't have a choice because the children didn't give me one. My continuing visits meant I had plenty of contact with children who'd been through the system again and again, and who had suffered through time served at Mt. Meigs. Some eventually trusted me enough to tell at least a little of their stories. A few were even willing to swear out complaints about being beaten. I heard the same stories often enough to know that they couldn't all be made up, but the people I relayed them to came to a different conclusion.

One was an official at the state Department of Pensions and Security, the agency responsible for the children at Mt. Meigs and the other training schools. He sent back each of my reports with a note that the complaint was unfounded. When I'd call to ask why, he'd always tell me that school officials assured him the child was a troublemaker or a liar, or both. Maybe he really did think kids would make it all up just to cause trouble, but as far as I could tell, nobody ever bothered to interview the children who made the complaints, much less other children or staff at Mt. Meigs.

I also expressed my concerns directly to Superintendent Holloway, but he never accepted responsibility for anything. I made specific note of a case from April 1967: Willie James Glover, a runaway from Mt. Meigs, was brought to our detention center badly bruised, "with skin broken in several places." He said a staff member at Mt. Meigs had beaten him with a hoe handle. I called Holloway, who came to my office and promised to investigate the matter thoroughly. I had no choice but to turn the boy over to him. I never heard another word about him from Holloway or any other official. Little more than a decade later, Glover was stabbed in an Alabama state prison. He survived and successfully sued the state for failing to protect him once again. As of 2009, he was a federal fugitive wanted for violating probation after attacking a mailman with a knife.

Whenever I asked Holloway about other beatings that children reported to me, he would change the subject and moan about how Mt. Meigs got only a tiny fraction of the money white schools received and plead that he couldn't afford to hire better teachers, or fix up the buildings, or do anything more than let things go on the way they were and had always been.

However, Mt. Meigs had once been a model facility. Its founding in 1906 was a triumphant achievement for the State Federation of Colored Women's Clubs, which worked long and hard to raise money to build a school that could give some hope as well as vocational training for troubled black youths. Originally known simply as the Reformatory School, Mt. Meigs made such an impression in a short time that the state took over funding in 1911. The great educator Booker T. Washington was so convinced of the school's excellence that he urged Alabama to open it up to "colored" delinquents from throughout the state. "We keep in close touch with this reformatory," he wrote in 1915, "and I know that it is doing good work for the boys who are there."

Three years later, a gangly twelve-year-old from Mobile named Satchel Paige was picked up for shoplifting a handful of costume jewelry and packed off to what had been renamed the Industrial

School for Negro Children at Mt. Meigs. He was kept there until he was nearly eighteen. Years later, he wrote:

> Those five and a half years there did something for me— they made a man out of me. If I'd been left on the streets of Mobile to wander with those kids I'd been running around with, I'd of ended up as big a bum, a crook. That's what happened to a lot of those other kids.

The Mt. Meigs that Paige describes does sound like a model school, where a real effort was made to identify the children's interests and talents, and where they got a solid education and training. Paige became leader of the school choir, a drummer in the marching corps—and a star pitcher on the school baseball team. The coach told him that if he worked hard, he might just make a living at it. He went on to become one of the best pitchers in baseball history, one of the few Negro League stars to break into the major leagues. He never forgot Mt. Meigs. In his autobiography, *Maybe I'll Pitch Forever*, Paige wrote:

> I know it may sound funny to talk about a reform school that way, but when you grow up as poor as me, a place like Mt. Meigs can be mighty warm and good.

Little more than a generation later, I knew that something about that place had gone terribly wrong, but I couldn't get anyone to listen, including the man responsible for committing children there. Judge Thetford's chambers were on the same floor as my office, but it seemed like a long climb uphill whenever I went to inform him of a new complaint about Mt. Meigs. He'd let me talk a while, then nod and thank me for telling him. Sometimes he'd add, "Good for you," but that was all. He never made any effort to find out the truth for himself. He didn't call the superintendent or any of his own powerful political cronies. He couldn't be bothered to get in his car and drive half an hour to see for himself what conditions were. He just kept on sending children to a place we all knew to be substandard at best.

I can't say the judge had no sympathy at all for those black children, but I know he saw no political advantage in adopting their cause—and his own interests always came first, as he revealed when a federal judge ordered Alabama to integrate its reform schools in the fall of 1968. Judge Thetford didn't try to hide his contempt when he announced that he had no intention of complying with the federal order. The local paper quoted him:

> I'm not going to send white boys to Mt. Meigs or Negro boys to [the white school at] Birmingham. I have to stand for reelection every six years, and integration is not popular. I don't understand how the federal government is going to control the judgment of juvenile court judges.

A man who believed he was wiser and more powerful than the federal government certainly wasn't going to stop sending children to Mt. Meigs because it was a bad place—and I couldn't stop taking them there. If I'd refused, I'd certainly have been fired—and what good would that do? The ride back grew longer each time, as I knew I'd left another child to join those ghostly ranks. It became clearer and clearer that one day soon, I'd have to do more than file another complaint. I would have to make a stand, as so many others across the country were doing for so many of their own reasons.

The spring and summer of 1968 were among the most socially tumultuous times in modern American history. Protests against the Vietnam War swept through college campuses and into city streets, as civil rights demonstrations veered sharply off the path of nonviolence and erupted into full-scale riots. When Dr. King stood up for striking garbage workers that April in Memphis, he was struck down by an assassin's bullet as he stood on a hotel balcony. Then in June, Bobby Kennedy was shot to death minutes after winning the Democratic presidential primary in California.

These developments were swirling when my secretary popped her head through the office doorway to announce that some girls wanted to speak to me about Mt. Meigs.

3

Into the Fray

At first, the appearance of five black girls at my door was a curiosity. As a boy's counselor, I didn't have contact with many female juveniles. I could easily have asked my secretary to just send them down the hall to one of the women probation officers and gone back to my paperwork.

But these girls had been very clear: they wanted to see the boss, and I was the boss. And when I heard that the subject was Mt. Meigs, I couldn't turn them away.

I can't tell you much about what they looked like, except that they were black and somewhere between fourteen and sixteen. I don't remember what they were wearing, but it wasn't party dresses or evening gowns. They were obviously poor children familiar with the detention system: they had all been recently released from Mt. Meigs.

I could see in their eyes that coming to see me hadn't been easy. They were scared, and their scars and bruises made it obvious why. I knew that youth detention could be a rough-and-tumble business, but it was obvious that these girls had been the victims of someone with malicious intent. I wanted to ease their fears as much as possible. I closed the door, sat quietly, and just let them speak.

What I heard in the next forty-five minutes has stayed with me for more than forty years. The girls took turns describing a nightmarish routine of hard labor, beatings, and sexual abuse. Worst of all was the experience of seeing their friend beaten so badly that she miscarried. What in the world was a pregnant teen doing there in the first place? What was any child doing in a place like that?

As I listened, I thought about my own children. I promised those girls that I would do everything I could to protect others from the abuse they described, but I didn't tell them how I would do that because I didn't know. I had been making trips to Mt. Meigs for seven years, and I had been making formal complaints for probably three or four years—and nothing had changed. I didn't consider telling Judge Thetford about the girls because I knew it would do no good. Another memo to some state official would have been just as useless, and an insult to the girls who'd put such trust in me. This time, I knew I would have to go outside the system to find a way around the blue-blood network that would always protect itself, even at the cost of children's safety.

As anyone who has ever worked in a bureaucracy can tell you, this is not an easy decision. Going outside—whether it's outside your company, or your agency, or your government—will always be considered an act of provocation, if not betrayal, by the people you work for and even by some of the people you work with. The whistle-blower runs the risk of having the whistle shoved down his throat. I was willing to take that risk, but there wasn't an obvious way to go about it. Alabama was a closed universe, and a small one. Even if I were willing to go to court, I might end up in front of Judge Thetford or one of his buddies. I needed advice, and I knew just the person who could give it to me. I decided to pay a visit to Ira De Ment.

That night when I got home, I told Sharon what the girls had told me, and she reacted as I had with shock and sadness. I told her about my plan to see Ira. I didn't want to put my career at risk without her support. She didn't hesitate for a moment.

I KNEW IRA ONLY as a good man I'd faced across a courtroom, but I realized as we spoke that day that he was a better man than I'd imagined. As soon as I began telling him my suspicions, he began telling me his. They were remarkably similar. He had his own sources—the children he'd been representing in detention—and I had mine. Between us, we already had a fat catalogue of evidence against the state, and plenty of ideas about how to fatten it more. He embraced the cause and made it clear I wouldn't have to hire him. He'd simply join me as a partner in this quest to save the forgotten children of Mt. Meigs.

I was eager to move ahead but still unsure how to go about it. I was by now well-versed in the legal foundations of crime and punishment, particularly as they applied to juveniles. But I was talking to an expert, so I was prepared to bow to Ira's ideas on strategy. I wondered aloud whether we'd have any success arguing on the basis of *parens patriae*, a common-law doctrine that translates to "parent of the country." Basically, it means the state has an obligation to act in the interest of children and others who can't be responsible for themselves. I thought the abuses at Mt. Meigs were clearly a violation of that basic concept. To my surprise, Ira didn't agree or disagree: he cheerfully admitted that he had no idea what I was talking about and acknowledged that I knew more about juvenile law than he did. I realized Ira wasn't some blowhard who needed to impress everyone as the smartest guy in the room. He wanted to win as badly as I did, and he'd never let his ego get in the way. We would be full partners in this venture, each contributing what he knew best.

Ira came to one fundamental conclusion early in our conversation: our only realistic legal option was to file suit in federal court. No matter which doctrine we argued, this was a case about basic civil and human rights—and no state court in Alabama had anything but the most dismal record on either front. Only the federal government had the power and the will to slash through the hard knots of racism and corruption that kept the children of Mt. Meigs bound and gagged. Even going to federal court was no guarantee of success. There were still plenty of federal judges whose actions and beliefs were no different from their state counterparts, while others were just reluctant to make a fuss in the states where they lived and worked. To win, we'd not only have to prepare a powerful case, it would have to land in the right courtroom.

We would be taking a risk in more ways than one. If going outside the bureaucracy was an act of betrayal, going to federal court or any federal agency would be viewed as treason by many of the people I knew. Most white folks in Alabama really believed George Wallace's blather about the "tyranny" of the federal government, even lots of people who were less racially venomous than he was. It was one thing to disagree among ourselves; it was quite another to go crying to the Yankees for help.

That night, I had another conversation with Sharon. I knew I wouldn't be the only one to suffer the blowback. I stressed again that I could be putting my career at risk, but I'd also be putting her at risk—and our children. Again, she didn't hesitate to give me her complete support. I knew Judge Thetford wouldn't be nearly as understanding, but that was okay because I had no intention of telling him anything about our plans. He had shown nothing but contempt for those children, as he had for all black people, and he'd given me no support in the past when I pursued complaints about Mt. Meigs. He was also very much a part of the political structure that had created the mess we were trying to clean up. I didn't know what he might do to sabotage our plans, but I couldn't take a chance.

So while I waited for Ira to prepare our suit, I simply continued counseling kids, filing paperwork, and overseeing the design and construction of the new detention center. Thetford had no real interest in the center's details, so I had a more or less free hand. It was shaping up nicely, too, with real classrooms, a chapel, and a full gymnasium with basketball hoops, as well as an outdoor sports field. At night, each child would sleep in a separate room on a mattress raised up on a concrete-shell bunk, instead of sprawled across the common floor. These were real improvements for the children as well as the staff. For myself, I picked out a nice, red carpet and plenty of bookshelves for my office. I was still an optimist then. I knew that Ira and I were heading into a storm, but I believed I would weather it and be around Montgomery for many years to come.

MEANWHILE, I SENT IRA all my files on Mt. Meigs, as well as a letter detailing my impressions of the place and laying out the predicament my office and Ira's clients both faced: our youth detention center was still overflowing with children who were stuck there for months on end while the state reform schools refused to accept them. But what if we managed to break the logjam? We'd only be sending many of those children to Mt. Meigs, where we knew they'd be abused.

Ira's solution was simple but ingenious: we could argue both cases at once and insist the court solve both problems. They were both urgent. He knew that even a larger county detention center wouldn't be suited for long-term confinement because it wasn't designed to be—and besides, the rehabilitation and education of juvenile offenders was the state's responsibility. Ira's strategy came into focus a little more sharply each time we met over the next several months. He concentrated on finding exactly the right case of the right children on which to build a claim. Unfortunately, the girls whose stories had spurred me to action weren't suitable because they were no longer in the state's care. We needed children who were currently trapped in county detention while awaiting transfer to Mt. Meigs.

We settled on five boys ages thirteen to fifteen who were in my custody. I don't know how Ira decided which one to list first on the lawsuit—it wasn't by age or alphabetical order—but Charles Stockton rose to the top. I don't remember Charles, and I don't know where he is today, but his name remains the emblem of our fight: *Charles Jerome Stockton, et al. vs. Alabama Industrial School for Negro Children, et al.*

I waited until the day before we filed our suit to face the steepest hurdle. I knew I had to tell my father before he heard it anywhere else. It was a conversation I looked forward to about as much as the time I had to tell him I'd dented the new car he bought for me. To my surprise, he took this news just about as calmly. He didn't bother to tell me he hated what I was about to do because that was obvious. Instead, he told me he'd support my decision because he knew I believed in what I was doing. This really shouldn't have surprised me. Throughout my life, my father supported me for doing what I thought was right, even when he disagreed with it. He was a man of honor.

THE BIG DAY CAME on Wednesday, January 22, 1969, when a court clerk officially stamped and recorded our case as Civil Action 2834-N in the United States District Court for the Middle District of Alabama, Northern Division. Legally, it was a lawsuit seeking relief from ongoing violations of the constitutional rights of those five boys and "all other minor Negro children similarly situated." But really, those nine legal-size pages amounted to an indictment of Alabama's segregated juvenile justice system in general, and the people who ran Mt. Meigs in particular. It named not only the school but the board of trustees and the school administrators, including E. B. Holloway, as defendants.

Our argument against holding children indefinitely in my crowded, windowless detention cells was identical to our argument against subjecting them to the brutality of Mt. Meigs: both were cruel and unusual punishment, which is barred by the Eighth Amendment to the U.S. Constitution. While both were unconstitutional, the abuse we demonstrated at Mt. Meigs was also unconscionable. The suit laid out everything we'd learned about Mt. Meigs being overcrowded, understaffed, and so poorly funded by the state that children were forced to work the farm for their very subsistence. We presented a portrait of a reform school that made a grossly inadequate attempt at teaching academics while offering only a tiny handful of students any exposure to vocational skills. The lack of heat, the open sewage, and the tumbledown dorms all became part of the court record. But we went farther to charge that this so-called school was actually a "penal institution," where children were "coerced and driven by uneducated and sometimes illiterate overseers." Rather than students, we called these children what they really were: inmates.

The abuse we cited was not limited to a few isolated cases, as we made clear by noting that

> virtually all the inmates . . . are frequently, severely and unjustifiably beaten around their heads and over their entire back, arms and legs with broom and mop handles and fan belts and some of the inmates are held down on tables and floors by others, stripped of their clothing and unmercifully beaten with said weapons and then further beaten in order to force them to stand up.

Blame could not be placed entirely on illiterate overseers. The suit charged that school administrators, including Holloway and girls' supervisor Fannie B. Matthews, also took part in the beatings.

The suit asked the court to declare Mt. Meigs "unfit" for its intended purpose and to order an end to all of its brutal practices. Simply put, we insisted that Mt. Meigs be raised to an acceptable standard of care and education or be shut down so that the children imprisoned there, as well as the others waiting to be transferred there, could be sent to other institutions.

News of the case dominated the next morning's *Montgomery Advertiser*. A boldface headline stretched across the top of the front page: "Suit Alleges Youths Beaten." I knew Judge Thetford couldn't fail to notice. I wondered if he'd be waiting for me when I got to work, but I didn't see him all day. I did get a note from him that afternoon in the intraoffice mail. The tone was clear from the introduction: "Dear Mr. Abbott . . ." The memo noted that I hadn't informed him of the suit before filing, and it quickly became even less friendly.

> You are . . . aware of the fact that I was informed of no incidence of child mistreatment at the State Training School at Mt. Meigs prior to the filing of this suit. The Family Court of Montgomery County has full authority to correct and punish incidences of child abuse and is the proper forum for such action.

He went on to say that he had placed great trust in me over the years, but that I had betrayed that trust by filing this suit.

In my previous dealings with Thetford, no matter how unpleasant, he had always been honest. Now he was lying about me, on paper. I instantly regretted that I had respected his confidence all those years and never made notes on our conversations about Mt. Meigs or mentioned his name in any of the complaints I forwarded to the state. The truth was that he knew all the essential facts about the beatings and other abuse at Mt. Meigs and had done nothing, but I couldn't prove that. I realized now that I should never deal with him off the record again, so I decided to respond in writing—and I remained most civil. I assured the judge that the suit was no reflection on him and that my actions were compelled by my conscience and sense of duty in the face of "an intolerable situation."

In the days to come, I found myself explaining my actions to a lot of people. Friends I'd known all my life thought I'd gone crazy when they heard what I'd done. One after another, they wondered aloud why I'd take such a risk for a bunch of black kids. People I didn't know so well were obviously thinking the same thing, even if they didn't say so. Neighbors walked back into their homes whenever I stepped into the yard. Shopkeepers I'd patronized for years turned their backs when I walked into their stores. Some people crossed the street to avoid coming eye-to-eye with me. My staff, thank goodness, didn't run away. In fact, several rushed into my office to express their support. The rest were at least civil. And my family was great, including Dad. Sharon and the children got the same cold-shoulder treatment I did whenever they left the house, but none complained.

I was prepared for a long siege. Ira had warned me that lawsuits move with glacial speed through the long process of discovery, depositions, and pretrial hearings even before an actual trial becomes so much as a glimmer on the horizon. But we both had confidence that Judge Frank M. Johnson Jr. would take no more time than he needed to make a fair decision. We could not have asked for a better judge, because there probably wasn't a better judge in any court in the country. There certainly wasn't a more courageous judge on the face of the Earth.

FEDERAL DISTRICT JUDGES DON'T often become famous, but Judge

Johnson was already known across the South. Today, he's one of the most admired American jurists of all time. Back then, he was one of the most hated. Judge Johnson had been at the center of nearly every important civil rights case in Alabama since the early 1950s, and he had upheld the law even when public opinion was strongly against him. It was Judge Johnson who ordered an end to the segregation of Montgomery's public swimming pools, the ones the city then shut down in defiance. He was also the judge who put an end to segregated buses, and not just on Montgomery's local bus line: he ruled for the Freedom Riders, barring the city and state from harassing them, and he mandated the desegregation of interstate bus lines as well as bus depots. Then in 1963, he issued the first statewide school desegregation order. He also ordered the governor and police to get out of the way of the protesters who marched from Selma to Montgomery, and he struck down the poll tax that Alabama had used for many years to keep blacks and poor whites out of the voting booths.

Judge Johnson gave black people hope, and he gave white racists fits. He was a native of Alabama and a man of impeccable integrity, but George Wallace raged against him as a "carpetbagging liar." As a result of his tough but honest rulings, Judge Johnson and his entire family endured continuing death threats. His elderly mother's house was firebombed. He lived for years under the constant protection of federal bodyguards.

Arguing our case before Judge Johnson did not guarantee we would win, but it did guarantee that the children we represented would get a fair hearing without any political interference. We knew that Judge Johnson would put their interests first. The first test of our faith in him came about two weeks after we filed, when the attorney for Mt. Meigs made a motion to dismiss the case. It's a routine step, and such a motion is rarely granted unless a suit is completely without merit, but neither of us had real confidence that this suit would have survived such a challenge in state court, or even necessarily in the courtroom of another federal judge.

In asking Johnson to dismiss the case, the attorney for Mt. Meigs argued that the suit should have been filed in Montgomery County Circuit Court, specifically before Judge Thetford. Attorney Maury Smith said Thetford told him no one, including me, had ever brought allegations of child abuse at Mt. Meigs to his attention, either formally or informally. He told the court that Thetford should have been "afforded an opportunity to inquire into these allegations," according to a news story on the hearing.

Wasn't it curious that the attorney for these accused child abusers would repeat in court what Judge Thetford wrote to me? I knew then that our suspicions had been correct: if we had taken this case to Judge Thetford, it would have vanished forever. It was also clear that Thetford would never admit the truth about our many conversations concerning Mt. Meigs. If he was comfortable enough with his lies to make them part of a federal court record, nothing would change his mind.

To our relief, Judge Johnson rejected the dismissal motion and allowed our case to proceed. He did throw us one curve, however. Because we hadn't named any county agency or officials as defendants in our suit, he was hesitant to hear our arguments against holding children indefinitely in county detention. He suggested we amend the suit, but the state suddenly discovered there was room at Mt. Meigs after all and admitted all five of the boys. Of course, Ira and I both worried about what lay ahead for them, but we were fairly certain that even the people who ran Mt. Meigs weren't stupid enough to do anything foolish under the eyes of a federal judge.

GETTING THE STATE TO back down and admit these children was a victory in itself. Now, thanks to Ira, our hand was about to

U.S. Accuses Alabama Of Abusing Children At Institution for Blacks

WASHINGTON (AP) — The
government Saturday accused
Alabama of operating a juvenile

tion of the law because of their
race and are denied liberty
without due process of law.

become even stronger. Three days before we filed suit, Richard M. Nixon had become president of the United States, and the new administration set about filling dozens of important positions. To my surprise and delight, Ira was Nixon's choice as our district's U.S. attorney. I knew Ira had the experience to be the region's top federal prosecutor because he'd been an assistant U.S. attorney before he went into private practice. It turned out he also had the political connections. He was a lifelong Republican in a state where white Republicans were then nearly as rare as polar bears: Nixon had finished dead last that fall among major candidates in the state, as Alabama voted overwhelmingly for the American Independent Party candidate, George Wallace.

It wasn't clear when—or whether—Ira would be taking on his new duties. Even before he was officially nominated, others were jockeying behind the scenes for a more conservative candidate, Montgomery attorney Robert E. Varner. When Ira's opponents failed to change the new president's mind, they tried to block Ira's confirmation by smearing him with the charge that he once represented some members of the Ku Klux Klan. Ira didn't try to refute the claim because it was true. Like many lawyers, Ira had represented all sorts of unpleasant characters. The result of this maneuvering was nothing more than a minor delay in Ira's confirmation.

But Ira had already taken advantage of his new pipeline to Washington by relaying word of our suit to a fellow Nixon ap-

pointee, Jerris Leonard. Leonard had been picked to head the
U.S. Justice Department's Civil Rights Division, which meant
he was in charge of enforcing myriad laws and court decisions
that local governments, and even entire states, were struggling
mightily to ignore. Asking Leonard to even consider opening a
new case right off the bat was probably a bit bold, but so was Ira.
When Leonard looked at the evidence we'd gathered, he alerted
the director of the FBI. Soon a team of agents was dispatched to
interview former inmates.

I had little contact with Judge Thetford over the next month
or two, as we limited our conversations to the minimum neces-
sary to conduct business. But I discovered that Thetford was
talking to others about me when I picked up the *Advertiser* on
April 14, 1969:

> Proposal Gives Judge Firing Power
>
> A bill that would have the chief probation officer of the
> Montgomery County Family Court serve at the pleasure of the
> presiding judge was introduced by Sen. J. J. Pierce.
>
> The Montgomery lawmaker said he introduced the bill at
> the request of Family Court Judge William Thetford.

Without warning, Thetford was trying to remove my job from
the merit system, which was Alabama's version of civil service. In
short, he wanted to be able to fire me at will, and I had no doubt
that he had the will. I was determined to fight back, but I wanted
to do my fighting in public. I issued a statement to the papers
that afternoon, accusing Thetford of using political pressure to
soothe his "ruffled feelings."

"If I lose my job because of raising questions about the
treatment of children, then it is a job that is not worth having
anyway," I said.

Thetford fired back with another memo the next day: "This is to advise that you are suspended for a period of fifteen days for deliberate and willful disobedience of instructions." What instructions? I knew Thetford was still riled about the suit, but his memo didn't say so. He didn't have to say anything at all, because he had the right to suspend me for up to thirty days without appeal. But in citing "willful disobedience," he was clearly laying the groundwork to fire me regardless of whether his pet bill passed the legislature. Fortunately for me, Thetford's scheme unraveled quickly. The bill that would have put my fate into his hands was killed by the local House delegation within days. Thetford certainly sensed that he had no support for such an obvious personal reprisal and backed away from the idea of firing me. He reduced my suspension to ten days, and I went back to work the following week.

I had plenty to do, as the new detention center was taking shape. We were planning for a late summer opening, despite the usual minor problems and contractor delays. The lawsuit was no distraction at this point, because we were basically in a holding pattern as both sides prepared their cases, with trial most likely in December. The good news for me was that Ira did not step aside when he started his new job in the spring. He felt confident he could keep an eye on the preliminary proceedings while settling in. Besides, who was going to tell the U.S. attorney to butt out of a case that involved potentially serious violations of federal law?

THE MONTGOMERY COUNTY YOUTH Facility finally opened in September. There was some carping, of course, as some people still thought we'd spent too much money to coddle a bunch of delinquents. But it was a great achievement for the entire community. It was a relief to be done with the planning and finally have a decent place to work with the children in our care, and I was obviously proud because I knew how much I'd contributed by raising the money and then making and executing the plan. I had a hand in almost every detail that made this center the equal of any in the country. You can imagine how I felt at the opening ceremony as I stood by while a plaque was unveiled dedicating the place to Judge William F. Thetford.

The money for the new facility had also paid for an expanded staff, including a full-time administrator. Now I had about forty people working for me and far less reason to worry about children escaping or getting hurt because there wasn't enough supervision. I could put more time and effort into helping my people do a better job of counseling Montgomery's youth and maybe diverting more of them from serious trouble. We took advantage of our nicely landscaped surroundings by having staff meetings outside when the weather was pleasant. We'd put folding chairs out along the recreation field and watch the children toss balls while we tossed around ideas. One of the best features of the new center was that it was a few miles outside of town, and Judge Thetford's chambers remained in the old downtown courthouse. I didn't stand much chance of running into him more than once a week when he drove out to the center to preside over youth court. Even then, we did our best to steer clear of each other.

The Mt. Meigs lawsuit had faded from the headlines by now, but it had won a prominent place on Jerris Leonard's agenda. The FBI's findings supported the charges Ira and I had made in our suit. Here's a sample from one FBI interview with a former Mt. Meigs shop instructor and maintenance supervisor, taken in April 1969:

> I have observed . . . numerous beatings to inmates with both fan belts and broom sticks on almost a daily occasion. Inmates would receive these beatings for such things as being

late to dinner; being noisy in the mess hall; attempts to escape; fighting; stealing, etc.

As the evidence mounted, so did the prospect of direct federal intervention. In early November, the Justice Department, represented by U.S. Attorney Ira De Ment, joined our suit as co-plaintiff. Now Mt. Meigs wasn't just being sued by five poor children from Montgomery, it was being sued by the United States of America. The Justice Department's brief largely repeated our original suit, but now the allegations bore the stamp of authority: instead of being signed by Denny Abbott, county probation officer, the government's complaint was signed by John N. Mitchell, United States attorney general. The front-page headline in the *Advertiser* the next morning screamed: "Mt. Meigs Called 'Penal Institution.'" The news was relayed by wire services to papers across the country. Readers of the *New York Times* were informed: "U.S. Says Alabama Beats Delinquents."

There was now no logical reason for the state to continue fighting us, or resist our efforts to gather evidence. Our side simply had too much firepower, and we had the truth. Our evidence included sworn statements from fourteen inmates who witnessed or experienced the abuse we described. We also had testimony from independent experts we'd brought in to examine Mt. Meigs, such as Jack Blanton, who ran Florida's training schools. Yet Judge Johnson had to repeatedly order Holloway and the trustees to produce the files, names, and even witnesses that the court requested. It turned out we weren't the only ones who felt there was a shell game going on. Soon after we filed suit, the State of Alabama quietly opened its own investigation of Mt. Meigs. Officials set out to interview a number of former inmates, but one address after another supplied by the school's administration turned out to be bogus. The investigators couldn't decide whether they'd been hoodwinked or whether the record-keeping at Mt. Meigs was incompetent.

By defending an indefensible institution, Alabama was just running up a needless legal bill and delaying improvements that were urgently needed. Maybe the bureaucrats I'd sent those memos to over the years really believed the children were lying then, but now they knew better. Even before the Justice Department formally entered the case, the commissioner of the Department of Pensions and Security had a report on his desk that substantiated our most serious charges.

A memo to Commissioner Ruben K. King dated September 9, 1969, informed him that Mt. Meigs was equipped to house 300 children but held 428, and had a "totally inadequate" social services department. The memo also quoted former employees who said girls were routinely subjected to an "extreme use of paddles" and often sexually assaulted by other inmates. Boys in the fields were left at the mercy of other students designated as overseers, who forced them into sexual submission. "This has caused an almost intolerable situation for the young children," the memo stated. "In one instance a child's rectum was severely lacerated by an older boy which necessitated medical treatment by a physician."

We had subpoenaed years of previous state inspection reports on Mt. Meigs and found nothing that even hinted of such cruelty. How could this violent abuse of children in the state's care escape the suspicion of state officials? Reading those annual reports, it's obvious that the children slogging through those fields were as invisible to Alabama's child-welfare officials as they were to the rest of the world. The inspectors were focused on filling in their forms with numbers and check marks, not on fulfilling their responsibility to safeguard those children.

We didn't specifically name the State of Alabama as a defendant in our suit, because its responsibility for Mt. Meigs was beyond question. As the Justice Department informed the court, Mt. Meigs was "a State-owned and controlled school, established and operated under (the state's) authority." But as our evidence showed, the state repeatedly failed to exercise that authority. No one at the state level had ever questioned Holloway's clearly inadequate credentials, nor those of his subordinates. No one asked why the girls at Mt. Meigs were placed under the supervision of a woman with no more than a high school diploma whose previous job was at a garment factory. Or why the boys in the fields were watched over by a man who'd never gotten past the fourth grade. The governor appointed trustees who never reported back to the state and never questioned or even reviewed the workings of the school. This was summed up for the record by my counterpart from Birmingham, A. C. Conyers, who was chief probation officer of Jefferson County's family court. In a response to the state's own report that became part of the court file, Conyers wrote, "There is absolutely no meaningful communication between the Board of Mt. Meigs and its Administration nor between the Administration and the state . . ."

The state kept its internal report secret for months. Its existence was revealed by Governor Albert Brewer when he told reporters during a press conference on Nov. 11 that a state investigation had shown "some cruel punishments may have been inflicted on prisoners" at Mt. Meigs. "Our report points out that many of the problems can be traced to the lack of trained social workers," he said, according to a story the next day in the *Birmingham News*. Brewer also conceded that some facilities at the school were inadequate and promised money for improvements.

But the governor's further remarks showed his reference to the children as "prisoners" was no mistake. He insisted that "some of the problems at the institute also stem from federal investigators who visited there. When the investigators came, inmates suddenly got the idea they didn't have to work any more," the governor said. "They're better off working." It was incredible that after all we'd shown in court—and after reading the state's own report—the governor of Alabama could blame federal investigators for the horrors of Mt. Meigs and suggest that these children were somehow responsible for being assaulted because they didn't work hard enough.

At that point, there was no way for the state to keep the report from becoming public and being entered into evidence, and once that happened, there wasn't much left for the state to defend. Amid a flurry of depositions and hearings signaling that the trial was approaching, Leonard flew in from Washington to huddle with Ira and the opposing attorneys. They all agreed to ask Judge Johnson for a delay while the state made an effort, at least, to fix Mt. Meigs. The judge agreed but made it clear that he'd better see progress quickly.

Within weeks, E. B. Holloway announced that he was retiring for "health reasons." Governor Brewer asked J. B. Hill, former superintendent of the boys' reform school in Birmingham, to come out of retirement long enough to set things right at Mt. Meigs. Hill agreed and took over the school on January 19. Almost as soon as he arrived, Hill asked to look over the school's financial records and discovered there were none: no budget, not even a ledger book. He did turn up $35,000 in unpaid bills, and not a dime to pay them. He had to ask the governor to send money to settle the school's debts.

CHANGE CAME RAPIDLY OVER the next several months. All the girls were transferred to other schools, and so were enough of the boys to cut the overall population to 110. Enough additional staff was hired to allow twenty-four-hour supervision of all children. The most dilapidated dorms were demolished, and boys were moved into former girls' housing, which was in better shape. New toilets were installed in the dorms—and Hill issued instructions for children and staff to wash up after using them when he discovered this wasn't common practice.

The farm was shut down so the boys could spend their days in class instead of in the fields. Real teachers were hired, too, as well as social workers. A part-time doctor was hired to give every child a medical exam on admission. For the first time, the staff received written procedures requiring new students to be evaluated and counseled by trained professionals. Welding, auto mechanics, masonry, and other trades were added to the vocational program.

Most important, Hill issued strict guidelines for corporal punishment—and warned that violations could result in immediate dismissal. It seems strange nowadays to talk about guidelines for hitting students, but paddling was legal then in Alabama's public schools, as it was in much of the country. What mattered most at Mt. Meigs was that there would be no more beatings with hoe handles and fan belts. Only fanny whacks with the prescribed pine-wood paddle were allowed, and only when justified. Each paddling had to be witnessed by at least one other staff member, and a report filed with the superintendent within twelve hours.

Every one of these steps was relayed to Judge Johnson, who set a timetable for more progress. He held Mt. Meigs under threat of trial for more than a year. In July 1971, he at last signed a final judgment in favor of the plaintiffs, meaning Ira and I had won our fight on behalf of the children of Mt. Meigs, with the help of the federal government. The judgment required all the improvements at Mt. Meigs to become permanent. By then, the transformation was remarkable. The school even got a new, shorter name: the

Alabama Industrial School. There was no need to add "for Negro Children" because Judge Johnson's final order required Mt. Meigs to accept "male juvenile delinquents between the ages of 15 and 18, without regard to race."

The case was finished, but not quite closed. Before Judge Johnson signed his final order, Ira put out the word that his office maintained an interest in Mt. Meigs' past as well as its future:

> U.S. Attorney Ira De Ment confirmed today he is "considering" prosecuting E. B. Holloway and his assistant, Fannie Matthews, for physical mistreatment of juveniles while they were in supervisory positions at the Alabama Industrial School for Negro Children at Mt. Meigs.

The story in the *Montgomery Advertiser* prompted a letter in defense of Holloway from a longtime Montgomery resident who was familiar with the school. "I have been made sick by the conditions I have seen at the Industrial School," he wrote to Ira. "I think it is a grave miscarriage of justice to make this man the goat for the callous attitude that the State of Alabama had toward this institution."

Ira replied that he had decided not to prosecute Holloway, but that the former superintendent's actions were inexcusable:

> I do not consider Mr. Holloway's lack of training or direction, or finances, or the fact that he was always understaffed, to be defensive of a cruel assault and battery on a defenseless child. Nor can I accept the argument that Mr. Holloway was a "product of the system."
>
> These same arguments could be made, and indeed were made, for the S.S. Guards at Dachau and the other Nazi concentration camps.

Ira went on to agree that the state bore responsibility for Mt. Meigs, but so did the community that looked the other way all those years. He wrote:

> My biggest and most genuine disappointment . . . is directed at the prominent and distinguished citizens who knew of the conditions at Mt. Meigs and who for whatever reason did nothing about them. To my knowledge, no one ever attempted to collect the facts, no one ever complained to the Governor, no one ever wrote a letter to the editor or to the Legislature, or to the Department of Public Safety, or made any complaint at all. Those who were "made sick by the . . . conditions at Mr. Meigs" apparently lacked whatever it takes to get people to stand up and be counted on a moral issue.
>
> I reiterate that unless I had filed a law suit and unless I had received permission from Denny Abbott to use his name as the plaintiff, in my judgment conditions at Mt. Meigs would be the same as they have been for the last "twelve" years.

Man behind reform

Denny Abbott brings change to Mt. Meigs

BY CAROL NUNNELLEY, News staff writer

In years to come, children who go to the state school for delinquents at Mt. Meigs will probably have no idea who Denny Abbott was.

IT'S VERY DOUBTFUL that there'll even be a bronze plaque on some obscure post to make them ask.

But if those youngsters at Mt. Meigs are getting a better break — as state officials have promised they will — some part of their thanks should go to Denny Abbott.

Abbott is the chief probation officer of Montgomery's juvenile court, who one day more than a year ago decided that his "normal" complaints about conditions at Mt. Meigs weren't working.

He made up his mind to try another, more controversial tack.

ABBOTT

Abbott found a lawyer and encouraged a suit on behalf of youngsters being sent to the rural campus, supposedly for rehabilitation but actually, Abbott believed, for neglect and sometimes outright abuse.

It was this federal court suit — filed first by Montgomery's Ira DeMent as a private attorney, continued later by him as a U. S. District Attorney on behalf of the U. S. Justice Department — that prompted formal, in-court promises by the state last week to make sweeping changes at Mt. Meigs.

LEARNING ABOUT Gov. Albert Brewer's actions last week, Abbott — who has to rank as one of the state's most outspoken critics of Alabama's policies at Mt. Meigs — was

4

Money Trumps Ideals

ost of the unpleasantness my family and I experienced as a result of filing the suit had passed before Judge Johnson made his ruling.

My complaints on behalf of black children might not have been popular, but they didn't inconvenience anyone we knew. Little by little, the neighbors quit running inside, and shopkeepers started waiting on us again.

The publicity I received as a result of the suit was almost entirely positive. The *Birmingham News* ran a particularly flattering piece:

> Denny Abbott Brings Change to Mt. Meigs
>
> In years to come, children who go to the state school for delinquents at Mt. Meigs will probably have no idea who Denny Abbott was.
>
> It's very doubtful that there'll even be a bronze plaque on some obscure post to make them ask.
>
> But if those youngsters at Mt. Meigs are getting a better break—as state officials have promised they will—some part of their thanks should go to Denny Abbott.

I had indeed already been thanked by a number of parents of black children in the detention system and others in the community. They let me know that they appreciated this rare example of a white public official reaching out across the color line to help. I got to thinking that I could accomplish even more in an elected office, and I figured some of the folks who had expressed their appreciation might just help me get there.

So as the Mt. Meigs suit was approaching resolution, I decided to run for a seat on the city commission in the March 1971 election. I took a leave of absence from my job and filed the paperwork to qualify for a place in the Democratic primary for public affairs commissioner, the official in charge of the then-all-white police and fire departments. By the time qualifying ended, there were seven candidates for the job, including the incumbent. I felt certain my reputation would help me carry the black vote. I knew I also had plenty of white supporters, including many of the folks who had joined me in passing the bond issue for the new detention center. With a little luck, I just might win.

I didn't have much money, but I did have a platform. I was quoted in the local paper promising "meaningful communication between the police and the young people of our city," with the goal of making each officer "an advocate, not an adversary." I took out an advertisement that urged Montgomery to "Vote

Denny Abbott Qualifies For Commissioner Race

Denny Abbott, Montgomery County's chief probation officer, today became the sixth candidate to qualify to run for public affairs commissioner in the March Democratic primary.

Incumbent Commissioner Jack Rucker, rumored a strong contender for state public safety director, said Tuesday he'll qualify late this week. The deadline is noon Saturday.

City-County Personnel Director Wade Moss said Abbott, a merit system employe, has been granted a leave of absence from Family Court to make the political race.

The leave began today and is in effect until March 22, the date of a Democratic primary runoff that seems inevitable in the crowded public affairs contest.

Abbott, 31, joined Family Court as a probation officer in October 1961. He was named chief probation officer in 1963.

In 1967, acting as a friend of the court in behalf of five black juveniles, Abbott filed a suit in Montgomery's U.S. Court against Mt. Meigs Industrial School. The action resulted in widespread reform at the reform school.

A Montgomery native, Abbott holds a 1961 bachelor's degree in sociology from Huntingdon College and a 1968 master's degree in criminology and corrections from Florida State University.

Abbott said his campaign will stress "establishing meaningful communication between the police and the young people of our city" so that the policeman will be regarded "as an advocate, not an adversary."

Other Democratic candidates who have qualified for the public affairs race are:

—Former Police Chief Drue Lackey, who resigned his Rucker appointment after a series of disagreements with Rucker.

—Michael T. Blacker, the first lawyer to run for a City Commission seat in many years.

—Dock H. Johnson, a former Montgomery police lieutenant and investigator for State Atty. Gen. MacDonald Gallion.

—Businessman Richard E. Hanan, a City Water Board member.

—Businessman John F. Rutherford, an unsuccessful candidate for mayor in 1967.

—RAYMOND MASSEY

Denny Abbott

for a Positive CHANGE." The ad stressed that I was a lifelong resident of Montgomery, a father of three, and president of the Dannelly School PTA, in addition to being chief probation officer and holder of a master's degree in criminology and corrections.

I had no campaign manager and no staff, but I had plenty of confidence in my powers of persuasion. I had a stack of flyers and campaign signs printed up, then talked to every group that would listen to me. I soon discovered that trying to do everything and be everywhere all by myself wasn't a perfect strategy. I was handing out flyers at a shopping center one afternoon and forgot that I was supposed to be speaking at a ladies' tea. When I didn't show up, one of the ladies called my house. My father happened to be there and answered the phone. He rushed over to take my place at the tea. The ladies loved him to death.

ELECT DENNY ABBOTT
PUBLIC AFFAIRS COMMISSIONER

THE QUALIFIED CANDIDATE
AND HIS FAMILY
Left To Right, Kim, Court, Sharon and Drew
★ Lifelong Resident of Montgomery
★ 9 Years Experience As Chief Probation Officer—Family Court
★ Holds Masters Degree in Criminology and Corrections
★ President of Dannelly School P.T.A.
★ Church Member—Mason and Shriner
VOTE FOR A POSITIVE... CHANGE!
Pd. Pol. Adv. by Denny-Abbott, Montgomery, Ala.

I felt awful when I realized what had happened. I got the name and address of every woman who'd been at that tea and sent each a note of apology asking her to forgive me. Luckily, they all did—but not everyone I approached during the campaign was so kind.

Running for office brought plenty of lessons in humility. It's hard to describe the feeling you get when you hand someone a campaign card and watch him take one glance and then toss it on the ground as he walks away.

The most valuable lesson came when it was time to meet with Montgomery's most influential black power brokers. The group distributed a ballot before each election highlighting its preferred candidates—and those candidates always won the black vote. I thought I was the obvious choice this time, as I offered the only hope for changing a police department that so many blacks regarded with fear and contempt. The incumbent, a retired cop supported by the city's establishment, certainly held out no such prospect.

I arranged a meeting at a restaurant owned by one of the members. They were seated at a table in the back when I entered, and one of them motioned for me to join them. I eagerly introduced myself and launched immediately into my campaign speech. I hadn't finished more than a sentence or two when one of the group interrupted me with a question: how much was I

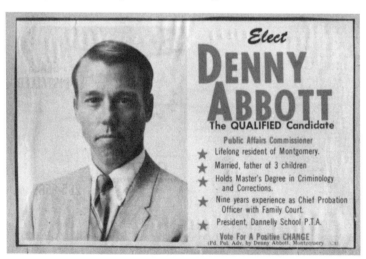

Elect
DENNY
ABBOTT
The QUALIFIED Candidate
Public Affairs Commissioner
★ Lifelong resident of Montgomery.
★ Married, father of 3 children
★ Holds Master's Degree in Criminology and Corrections.
★ Nine years experience as Chief Probation Officer with Family Court.
★ President, Dannelly School P.T.A.
Vote For A Positive CHANGE
(Pd. Pol. Adv. by Denny Abbott, Montgomery ...)

prepared to pay them? I was stunned. I'd been hoping they'd donate to my campaign. Instead, I was being asked for a payoff. When I told him my campaign was basically broke, he told me the meeting was over.

The members made their choice clear on the ballot they distributed before election day: they endorsed the incumbent, who was reelected. Of the seven candidates, I finished fourth. So much for youthful idealism. I went back to my job as chief probation officer and never so much as thought about running for office again.

5

A Home for Every Child

I'd lost an election, but I hadn't lost my passion for my job or for children.

I continued my speaking schedule—not for votes or for money, but to keep children's issues in the public eye. The big issue for me was the drive to create a statewide youth authority. Without one, I couldn't see any real progress in giving children throughout the state a fair chance at a decent life. My not-so-secret ambition was to be in charge of such an agency.

Looking back, I realize it was a pipe dream. But one way or another, I was determined to be a force in improving the lives of Alabama's children. If the best way to do that was to continue being chief probation officer, that was okay with me. Judge Thetford and I had settled into a sort of détente. He may not have liked me, and he certainly didn't share my ideals, but he recognized my administrative skills and seemed pleased with my work. Nothing I had seen in my travels while planning the new detention center had convinced me I'd be any happier elsewhere. I might have retired in that job, and I'd almost certainly still be living in Montgomery, if I hadn't been quite so diligent in studying the detention reports the day Emmett Player turned up in 1972.

Emmett had been picked up after escaping from Mt. Meigs, and he'd be going back as soon as we could get him there. I was about to flip a page when the dates next to his name caught my attention. Emmett was fifteen years old, but the report showed he'd been at Mt. Meigs for five years. That didn't make sense. Mt.

Meigs didn't accept children under twelve, and children were rarely kept there longer than a year. I could have assumed the entry date was a mistake, but I picked up the phone instead and called Ed Grant, the twenty-four-year-old school principal who'd recently been appointed superintendent at Mt. Meigs. He told me there was no mistake, at least not in the records. I immediately sent for Emmett while I started making other phone calls.

What I learned sickened me: Emmett had been locked away for five years for no reason except that he was a black child without a home. He had done nothing wrong. No one had accused or even suspected him of committing a crime. Emmett simply had the bad fortune to be ten years old when his mother died in 1967. His father was in prison, and the police in Birmingham couldn't find anyone else who'd take him. So without consulting a judge or a social worker, they put Emmett in a car, drove him a hundred or so miles to Mt. Meigs, and left him at the mercy of an institution for delinquent children.

I hated the idea of sending him back there, so I started making calls to every place and everyone I could think of for help. I quickly realized there was a gaping hole in my knowledge of children's issues. I knew everything about delinquency but almost nothing about children who depended on the state because they were orphaned or otherwise without a suitable home. I learned that most of the children's homes in Alabama were run by churches, and the vast majority were for whites only. Few homes accepted black children, and the need far outstripped the availability.

I knew it wouldn't do any good, but I went and told Judge Thetford about Emmett. Predictably, he had no reaction. He dealt with dependent children all the time, so he wasn't surprised about the lack of facilities for blacks. He expressed no concern, about Emmett or any of the rest.

I called everyone I could think of at the state Department

of Pensions and Security, which had responsibility for placing children in homes. They not only knew all about the shortage of homes for black kids, they knew all about Emmett. They'd tried to find a place for him several times but had given up. Everyone I talked to about Emmett offered the same advice: forget about him, he's black.

The problem was that I couldn't forget about him, not with everything I knew about Mt. Meigs and what he must have gone through all those years. I had to help Emmett, but I couldn't without getting advice from someone who knew the law and could tell me whether these homes could legally turn him away. There was really only one choice, now that Ira De Ment was no longer in private practice. Howard Mandell was one of the few lawyers within shouting distance of Montgomery who worked on civil rights cases. He was a Yankee, but he was a smart Yankee—and a pretty cool young guy who had a passion for justice. He had graduated from Georgetown University Law School just two years earlier, in 1970, and had come to Montgomery to clerk for the judge he most admired: Frank Johnson, the man who had created such a furor among segregationists and who presided over the Mt. Meigs suit. He went on to help Morris Dees get the Southern Poverty Law Center started, which told me he had courage as well as brains.

Howard advised me to fill out applications to the homes that had turned us down, including those run by churches. If they rejected Emmett in writing, we'd have the basis for a federal lawsuit. I thought: Uh-oh. I did not want to get into another fight—believe me, I didn't. I sat there thinking: Why is this happening to me? Why couldn't this kid have turned up in Selma, or Mobile, or back in Birmingham, instead of in Denny Abbott's detention center?

I knew that plenty of children in similar circumstances undoubtedly had turned up in those places, and no one bothered to help them. That night, I had another talk with Sharon. She agreed there was no choice. So the next day, I started filling out the application forms, and I sent them to each place on the list. The results were exactly as expected. Every home turned us down, and most were clear about the reason: no blacks accepted.

Howard and I kept expanding the list, but the results didn't change. We discovered there were seventeen licensed children's homes in the state, all privately owned. Only four admitted blacks, and only two of those were even partially integrated. The imbalance was overwhelming: the all-white homes held a total of 750 children. The all-black homes held just 40.

We zeroed in on six homes that accepted children from throughout the state rather than just from their counties. All six were entirely white, even though three had stated in writing that they complied with the 1964 Civil Rights Act. Our legal argument was simple: although the law didn't require the integration of strictly private facilities, it did outlaw discrimination by government agencies and contractors functioning on behalf of the government. These homes all accepted children referred by the state, and they accepted state assistance. Clearly, they were performing a public function, and we were prepared to ask a court to hold them to the same standard as a public agency.

I thought I was being discreet as Howard and I compared notes over the next few months, but Montgomery always was a small town, and word got back to Judge Thetford that I'd been seen coming out of Howard's office. The judge didn't bother to ask what I was up to. He called me and two other supervisors to a meeting in his chambers one afternoon in September 1972 and told us that no one was to file any lawsuit of any kind without first informing him. I should have kept my mouth shut, but that's not me. I asked if his order meant I'd need his permission to get divorced. The judge didn't see the humor. Of course, we all knew he'd never give any of us permission to file any lawsuit of any kind.

I never considered telling him about my plans to sue on behalf of Emmett. I was already running into a wall of opposition from the state and had no doubt that Judge Thetford's cronies were keeping him informed and asking for his help in keeping me at bay. I'd even been shut out from talking to Emmett, who had been returned to Mt. Meigs; the superintendent turned me away when I went there to tell Emmett about our plans. Above all, Judge Thetford would never consent to any attempt to integrate children's homes—or any other facility, public or private. In fact, I was certain he would try to stop me, but I was convinced he had no legal right to interfere. I felt sure this suit would not affect the operation of his court in any way, so his order didn't apply. Nor did I consider it a legal order. Access to the court system was my constitutional right, and this suit wasn't even about me. In short, Judge Thetford's order didn't cause me a moment's hesitation.

On Friday, November 17, 1972, Howard and I filed a federal suit in the names of Emmett and two other boys who also desperately needed a home. Both were black and had been living at a school that closed after the Catholic priest who founded it was killed. The state sent the boys to live with elderly relatives who were physically and financially incapable of caring for them, because there was no other place to put them. The main target of our suit was the Department of Pensions and Security, the state agency responsible for Alabama's social welfare programs and the same one I'd tangled with over Mt. Meigs. We also named the six all-white homes we'd identified, including three church-owned facilities: the Alabama Baptist Children's Home in Troy, the Presbyterian Home for Children in Talladega, and the United Methodist Children's Home in Selma. The suit was filed as a class action, which meant we were asking the court to open those homes to every child who needed a place, regardless of color. We got a lucky break almost immediately when the case was assigned to Judge Johnson. That hadn't been a sure thing; there were two judges in our district.

News of the suit hit the papers the next day, and the reaction was powerful and swift. First thing Monday, Judge Thetford called me into his chambers and fired me. It was a strange scene. His secretary was already seated with her notebook out when I arrived, and the judge asked me to sit while they finished their work. I listened as he dictated my letter of termination.

"Dear Mr. Abbott," he began. "Within the past month, I instructed you . . . that there were to be no suits filed by any personnel of the Montgomery County Youth Facilities without my prior knowledge and approval."

After each paragraph or so, he'd interrupt to ask me if the facts were correct. I had to admit they were. It was true, as he went on to state, that I had filed a suit and that I had done so without consulting him. His letter never said my suit affected the operation of his court, or I'd have contested that.

He concluded with, "This discharge is effective immediately. Yours very truly, William F. Thetford."

And that was that. After eleven years, I was no longer an employee of the Montgomery County Family Court. Just that quickly, I went from chief probation officer to unemployed father of three. I walked back to my office, cleaned out my desk, and said good-bye to my staff. I can't say I didn't expect this, but I sure didn't like it. Before I left, I dictated a letter of my own to Judge Thetford and the court. "I believe that my dismissal is unjust and amounts to a political reprisal," I wrote. "I do not accept my dismissal and I will fight it through every legal channel."

I was already thinking about the next court fight when I got home. Sharon took the news well, but she also had news of her

For Parentless, Homeless Blacks

Suit to Integrate Orphanages Brings Woe to a Chief Probation Officer

By J. M. McFadden
FROM MONTGOMERY, ALA.

The chief probation officer for Family Court here in Alabama's capital city found himself out of a job after he filed a Federal suit to desegregate orphanages in the state.

Denny Abbott, who had held the top Family Court post since 1963, was fired by state Circuit Judge William Thetford, his superior, for "flagrant and willful disobedience of orders." Abbott hadn't told Thetford about the suit ahead of time. Thetford says he told Abbott "within the past month . . . that there were to be no suits . . . without my prior knowledge and approval." And he says he learned about the current suit in a newspaper story.

In 1969 Abbott filed a Federal suit that brought about a complete reorganization of the state's reform-school system. All-black juvenile workhouses with a history of physical abuse were converted to desegregated schools under close court supervision. After that incident, Thetford suspended Abbott for 15 days and attempted unsuccessfully to have a law passed to remove Abbott's job from the protection of the civil-service system.

Abbott filed the current class action for three black youngsters who, he says, have no place to go in Alabama. One of them,

Emmett Player, 15, has been in reform school for five years because his father is in prison and his mother has disappeared. The other two youths are living with elderly relatives unable to provide proper care. The suit seeks to force segregated private institutions that accept state aid to accept black children also, or to establish public facilities for homeless children.

Although church-sponsored orphanages were among the defendants in the suit, several church groups have circulated petitions supporting Abbott. And his lawyers amended the suit to ask the state to end the tax-exempt status of segregated orphanages. New defendants are the state Department of Revenue and its commissioner. Abbott says that tax exemptions for these private institutions deprive the state of money that could provide public homes for children. Officials attempting to place neglected children often find that orphanages have waiting lists. Comments Abbott: "There's a chance if he's white; none if he's black."

Abbott says he wants his job back, "and I will fight to get it" through action of the personnel board or the Federal court. He envisions a $6 million plan to provide aid for delinquents as well as neglected children. "Any time the system is challenged, the political boat begins to rock," Abbott says. "I think it's time somebody got wet."

own: people had been calling since early morning with ugly words and even threats. I got a taste almost immediately. Some callers said they were from the Klan and they were going to teach me a lesson. Just about all of them called me a "nigger lover." The only callers who troubled me were the ones who mentioned my family. I couldn't help but worry about the kids. We all talked that night, and I told them I wasn't going to back down. I'm proud to say none wanted me to. In the days that followed, I think each was confronted in some nasty or threatening way—and none backed down either.

This was different from the reaction to the first suit. This time, people were downright mean instead of just rude, and I understood why. Nothing riled white folks like the threat of integration, even though they weren't the ones being integrated. To so many whites, integration was a fighting word as well as a profanity. You didn't say it, much less do it—and you certainly didn't even think about asking the federal government to order it. But we'd gone beyond even that. In Alabama, suing the Baptist church was like suing God—and we'd taken on the Presbyterians and Methodists at the same time.

I can't honestly say any of this was unexpected. I surely knew Judge Thetford would fire me if he ever got the chance. So you might assume I had a backup plan—either another job in the wings or a fat savings account to fall back on. Sadly, no. I had no plan at all except to get my job back. I know this may sound a little odd. Why would I want to go back to work for a man like Judge Thetford? The short answer is because I had three children to feed, but I also wanted vindication. I truly believed then, and I believe now, that I did nothing wrong, and I could not accept being punished unjustly. Within three weeks of my firing, Howard and I filed a motion asking the court to hear my plea for reinstatement as part of the Player case.

We were reluctant to file it as a different suit, because it might be assigned to a different judge, and we had reason to be more than a little leery of the only other judge in the federal district. Robert E. Varner, whose friends had tried to maneuver him into the U.S. attorney's office instead of Ira De Ment, won an even bigger prize when President Nixon appointed him to the federal court in 1971. Varner's inside connection to Nixon was a fellow Alabamian, Winton Blount, the postmaster general. Blount was a successful businessman whose great legacy to Montgomery is the magnificent Blount Cultural Park, now scene of the Alabama

Shakespeare Festival. Getting Varner a seat on the federal bench does not rank as quite so glorious an accomplishment. Varner proved to be an undistinguished jurist with a high reversal record and a clear reluctance to rock the boat when it came to civil rights. Worse, from my perspective, he was an old fishing buddy of Judge Thetford.

While we waited for the court to rule on the motion, great news broke: state investigators had gone to Atmore State Prison to speak with Emmett Player's father. He told them he had a sister and where to find her. It turned out she had no idea where Emmett was all that time and was willing to take him in. Just that quickly, Emmett got a home with his aunt—the home he might have had all those years if anyone had bothered to ask a few simple questions. Unfortunately, this didn't signal a change of heart by authorities in Alabama's child-welfare system, as there were no changes in policies or procedures regarding other black kids. Most likely, state officials thought placing Emmett with his aunt would take the steam out of our case. If so, they were wrong. Finding a home so quickly for Emmett only strengthened my conviction that we were on the path to ensuring a home for every child in Alabama who needed one.

Nearly everything I hoped for had come my way in two federal cases until now. It was probably too much to hope for that to continue, as I learned when Judge Johnson ruled on my plea to get my job back. It would have to be filed as a separate case, and that case would be heard by Judge Varner.

6

The Long Good-bye

I'm in my seventies now and retired, but I still kick up a fuss now and then. I guess I'm just the kind of person who always has to feel he's trying to accomplish something worthwhile. So it's a good thing I had two court cases to fight after getting fired. They became my jobs, and I was determined to succeed at both of them. If Judge Varner was a hurdle we couldn't clear, then we'd just have to find a way around him—and we almost did.

The law provides a remedy for anyone facing a judge with a clear conflict of interest. You can file a motion to recuse, asking the judge to step aside and let someone else hear the case. Problem is, some judges take these things personally because basically you're challenging their ability to make a fair decision. Worst case, the judge turns down your motion and you have to argue your case before a guy who thinks you've attacked his integrity. To our surprise, Judge Varner raised the issue before we did. At a hearing in his chambers in early December, the judge told attorneys for both sides about his relationship with Thetford and actually suggested that Howard file a motion to remove him from the case. It was a great relief for us.

We were surprised, to say the least, when he turned down our motion barely a week later. "A judge cannot take lightly the burden he places on his fellow judges when he recuses himself," he explained.

What hogwash! I had no doubt then or since that Thetford was behind this, either directly or through an intermediary. I know it's hard to pressure a federal judge, because they're appointed for life, but Thetford didn't have to twist the judge's arm. Not only did he have their friendship to fall back on, but one of his lawyers was Judge Varner's former law partner. I don't know if they hashed it all out over dinner at the country club or over a few bourbons in the parlor of a mutual friend's home, but I wound up facing the same sort of stacked deck that would have doomed our suit if we'd filed it in state court.

Howard questioned the judge's apparent change of heart, but all Varner would say was, "While I can't be positive, I think I can be fair." We were both positive he meant exactly the opposite, but we were just beginning to learn an important lesson about the way Judge Varner conducted himself. He liked to have important conversations like this in his chambers, with no court reporter present to take notes. Howard repeatedly asked for one, but the judge always turned him down. This made him very difficult to challenge, and the harder Howard tried, the nastier things got.

At one hearing close to trial, Judge Varner launched into a personal tirade against Howard, accusing him of soliciting business by recruiting the two boys who joined Emmett in suing the state. This was a serious charge that could have had serious consequences for Howard, but it wasn't true. The boys' plight had been brought to Howard's attention by the folks from the shelter where they'd been living, and it was ludicrous to accuse him of stirring up business when he wasn't being paid a dime. Besides, that was all part of the suit before Judge Johnson. What did any of it have to do with my plea to get my job back?

Varner backed down from his accusations when Howard aired them in open court, but he still refused to step aside. What this episode really revealed was that Judge Varner's sympathies lay with all the others who wanted us to lose our fight to integrate the children's homes—and who were increasingly worried that we were going to win. Just days before the judge's outburst, we got a major boost when Judge Johnson invited the Justice Department to step in as a friend of the court. Once again, the racists were going to have to beat the United States, not just little old me.

If there was anything good at all about Judge Varner, it's that he didn't dawdle. I wanted a quick trial so I could get back to work. He obliged by scheduling trial for mid-January 1972, and he stuck to it. The fireworks started as soon as I took the stand the first day. Just about every time Howard asked a question, one of the defense attorneys would object, and Judge Varner would agree with him. No matter how Howard rephrased the question, the judge would interrupt and insist he'd already told him not to ask it. At one point, he threatened to hold Howard in contempt, and I thought there was no way to avoid watching my attorney get dragged off to jail. But somehow, Howard and the judge both managed to cool down, and I managed to make the key point of our case. I testified that Thetford had ordered the staff to file no lawsuits of any kind without his consent, which was not only unreasonable but to my mind illegal.

The second day was devoted mostly to Judge Thetford's testimony, which Judge Varner seemed to find far less objectionable than mine. I think the only completely honest statement my former boss made on the stand, other than spelling his name, was when he was asked if he would have given me permission to file the Player suit if I'd gone to him first. He said: no. The rest was fiction. He said his order never applied to all suits but only to suits that might affect his court, which sounded far more reasonable than the truth. He said his biggest concern about my suit was that it might end up hurting the poor, homeless black children of Montgomery. He had been working tirelessly—behind the scenes, of course—to help raise money for a home for these very children, but all the publicity about my suit had made that all but impossible now. It's a wonder the poor man could keep from sobbing.

There was no jury, so there was nothing left except for Judge Varner to rule. He gathered the attorneys in his chambers once more and indicated he'd be calling them back in a few weeks to hear his decision. But before adjourning, he gave them a remarkably candid glimpse at his thinking. Again, no court reporter was present, but Howard later recounted the judge's remarks for the record: "Gentlemen, while I do not plan to set this reason forth or discuss it in my opinion, it appears clear to me that the reason Judge Thetford took the steps he did was that the lawsuits filed by Mr. Abbott are not generally popular and Judge Thetford was concerned about his reelection. He didn't want Denny filing any more of those kind of lawsuits."

Howard immediately moved to enter the judge's comments in the trial record, but Judge Varner turned him down, and he ordered Howard's motion sealed, too. They wrangled for a couple of weeks, as the newspapers carried stories about "secret documents." Finally we prevailed, and the judge let it all be heard in open court. Now everyone in Montgomery knew Thetford's real motive, and they knew he lied about it. They also knew Judge Varner hadn't been fooled. How could any judge rule against me under those circumstances? I felt certain I'd be strolling across that familiar red carpet to my old desk one day soon.

I found out how wrong I was on February 20, 1973. "Varner Upholds Firing of Abbott," the local paper reported. As I read Judge Varner's ruling, his words stung more than his conclusion. Referring to me, Varner wrote: "His lack of consideration for his employer and for his job are his undoing." I was furious at that. My employer, after all, was the public, and my job was to look after Montgomery's most troubled children. Nobody who knew what I'd done and what I'd sacrificed could possibly question my dedication to either, but there it was in writing for all the world to read.

We immediately appealed the decision, but appeals take time, and I didn't have much time left before I'd have to dust off my old squirrel gun and go hunting for supper. Not only had I fully expected to get my job back, I was counting on getting a hefty check to make up for back pay with interest. Instead, I had to borrow one thousand dollars against my life insurance to pay the bills while I searched for another job. Thank goodness I had that to fall back on. I was certain a man with my experience and credentials could land something decent before it ran out. Of course, I was wrong again.

My dream was still to run a statewide youth authority, and now there seemed to be a chance that the legislature would create one, thanks in part to the problems our lawsuits had brought to light. I called on everyone I knew—and a bunch more I didn't know—to lobby for the top job. I guess it's fair to say I was made to feel about as welcome as an IRS auditor. It was the same no matter what job I applied for anywhere in state or local government. I even applied to take over Mt. Meigs when I read that the latest superintendent resigned after auditors started questioning where all the money was going. If there was any mess I was clearly qualified to clean up it was that one, but I didn't even get an interview.

The only person willing to pay me to clean up anything was an old friend, Ben Ellis, who had a bumper-chroming shop in Montgomery. He hired me to clean the bathrooms and the stockroom. I made deliveries, too. The few dollars he paid me helped more than he knew. It's a cliché, but you really do find out who your real friends are when times are hard. I found out I had more friends than I knew.

As soon as I was fired, two members of my staff quit in protest.

Dozens of people, including many I'd never met, wrote letters to the court urging that I be reinstated. Others wrote directly to me, offering words of encouragement. Some of this support came from professional groups, like the Alabama Psychological Association and the state chapter of the National Association of Social Workers. I also heard from ministers, from mothers of boys I'd counseled, and from complete strangers who'd simply read about what I had done in the newspaper and wanted me to know they were on my side. A group of church women got up a petition demanding that I be rehired so I could continue working "in behalf of poor and needy children." None of this meant anything to the people who were determined to drive me out of Montgomery, but it meant the world to me. Sure, I'd have been happy if someone called to offer me a job, but I was deeply touched when black mothers called to offer me their food stamps.

My family and I struggled through that summer, but we scraped by thanks to a couple of temporary jobs: I taught a summer class at Auburn University, and I conducted a study of Alabama's jails for the Children's Defense Fund. By then I knew I had no chance of finding another job in criminal justice or social services anywhere in Alabama, so I widened my search across the country. I still have a file containing copies of the letters I mailed. It looks like the Manhattan phone book. Only a few of my queries got more than a lukewarm response, despite my clear qualification for the jobs and some impressive recommendations, such as a letter from U.S. Senator Edward M. Kennedy of Massachusetts, who was a friend of a friend. I finally managed to get interviews in St. Louis, New Jersey, Virginia, and a few other states, but each ended the same way. Sooner or later, I'd be asked why I sued my own state. My answer never seemed to matter.

After being out of work nine months, I had to consider the possibility that my hard-earned professional credentials might be as worthless as Confederate money. I was nearly at a loss about where to turn, when I got a call from O. J. Keller, head of Florida's Department of Youth Services. Jack Blanton, the fellow who came up from Florida to inspect Mt. Meigs as part of my lawsuit, had told him about me. Keller wondered if I'd be interested in running a regional detention center program based in West Palm Beach.

I didn't have to think very hard about it.

7

Starting Over

My new boss in Florida had one request: please don't sue us unless you talk to me first. In return, he promised he'd listen to any complaints and try to fix any problems I brought to his attention.

The poor guy got an earful.

Like most people, I didn't really hear the "West" in West Palm Beach. It sounded impossibly rich and tropical, and in some ways it has always been both. Today, it's a city with an impressive skyline where you'll often see valets jockeying Bentleys and Aston Martins to and from upscale shops and restaurants. But drive a few blocks inland and you'll see what remains of the place I first saw in 1973, where houses, cars, and people all seem to slump under the weight of all that humidity.

Here's the really strange thing about West Palm Beach: it has no beach. It's cut off from the Atlantic Ocean by the real Palm Beach, an island of magnificent and glittering estates just across a thin strip of water known as the Intracoastal Waterway. The island and the ocean beyond might as well be a thousand miles away for most working folks, except for rich people's servants. The latter made up a good portion of the early population, along with merchants, shippers, and everyone else whose business depended on the farms that still stretch halfway across the state from the city's western fringe. Head that way and you'll find yourself standing on incredibly fertile soil called muck. It's so soft you can poke your whole hand down into it without trying very hard, and it's so moist and dark you might think you've struck oil. You wouldn't be entirely wrong, because soil that rich would have to make someone a fortune. But just like back home, it's never been the people working the fields who got rich. What I saw when I drove across the western reaches of Palm Beach County wasn't so different at all from rural Alabama: ramshackle houses and poor, tired people struggling in the hot sun.

The poverty out in what's called the Glades is even worse for many people because many small farms have gone under. And just as in Alabama, the folks who endure this poverty are disproportionately black. You may not think of Florida as the South in any sense except geography, but it was—and in many ways, it still is. Legal segregation was over by the time I arrived, thank goodness, but the racial contrast in housing, schools, and general prosperity was as clear as the Florida sky. There was plenty of anger, too, and not always below the surface. So it shouldn't have been a surprise that Florida was no more advanced than Alabama in providing social services, particularly for young people in trouble. The surprise was that in some ways, it was worse.

As regional director, I had jurisdiction over several youth detention centers spread out across 150 miles. The one at my new home base in West Palm Beach was the worst I'd ever seen, including the one I'd fought so hard to replace in Montgomery. The interior was cramped, drab, and lacking even basic equipment. The recreation yard was even worse—a pit with a sand floor and wire mesh around the top and sides. It looked like the sort of cage where they have illegal dog fights. I got a thermometer and tested the sand, and it read something like 120 degrees. How could I lock children in there?

I started pushing for a new facility almost from the day I arrived. And no, I didn't threaten to sue. My new bosses were at least interested in hearing my thoughts, and they supported my

Staff Photos by Peter Silva

Officials, Candidates and Other Visitors Tour the State's Juvenile Detention Center

Palm Beach Post 8-16-74

Politics Invade Detention Center

Director Wants Officeholders To See Dilapidated Conditions

By CAROL DUNLAP
Post Staff Writer

It was open house yesterday at the state's Juvenile Detention Center in West Palm Beach and Denny Abbott, the center's director, was a little nervous about his guest list.

Abbott invited a full roster of current and aspiring local officeholders to view the detention facility which, he says, badly needs renovation or replacement. But the detention official has met few politicians during less than a year at the center, so he was apprehensive about getting their names right.

He needn't have been.

By 1 p.m. the crafts room at the center on Australian Avenue was bustling with name tags ("Elect Cruikshank"); badges (Florida Highway Patrol, Marine Patrol), several faces newly familiar to Abbott from campaign billboards, and at last one bumper sticker ("Pick Cotton" — Donna Cotton, that is) stuck to a purse.

The overflow crowd also included a county commissioner, a state representative, several judges and bureaucratic administrators, and a large contingent from the League of Women Voters.

Opening the event, Ab-

Denny Abbott (Left) and Ansel Jefferies Answer Questions

pointed out, "kids who grew up in Palm Beach County and committed crimes in Palm Beach County and became a tax liability in Palm Beach County. They don't have 'State of Florida' stamped on their foreheads."

Robert Johnson intro-

talk to you about that land," Abbott replied, smiling.

Andy Andrews, candidate for the state House, recalled when juveniles were detained in a barracks at the old county airport. "The kids have no right to bail?" he asked. "Then

other aspiring state representative, asked what happens when the facility gets more kids than it can handle ("we've got to put them somewhere"); and incumbent Rep. Don Hazelton wanted to make it absolutely clear that "we're talking about money, in-

what the state told us to do," Jefferies charged, "but the state has changed its mind several times. There are no state standards."

"Is the county aware that there is no kitchen here?" a member of the League of Women Voters interrupted. Jefferies began to answer when Andrews broke in to head off a debate between Jefferies and Abbott.

"Let's just get a good facility," Andrews said, "and then if you're not doing a good job we can fire you both."

While some of the most vocal participants in the pre-tour discussion made their excuses to leave, the rest of the assembled officials and guests set off on a guided tour of the center inspecting bunk beds, sanitary facilities, barred cells.

Checking out the kitchen, several mothers from the League of Women Voters expressed concern that the youths in detention don't get enough to eat.

By 2:30, all but a few stragglers had left, and the center staff took a few minutes to wind down from the excitement of the afternoon.

"Say, why do you suppose that guy came from the Florida Marine Patrol?" one staff member asked. Another center idea of building something better based on all I'd learned. Of course, they left it to me to get the money. With their blessing, I launched the same sort of campaign that had worked before, talking to women's groups and anyone else who'd hear me. I'd learned how to get attention from the press, and I used that to my advantage, too. Florida politicians turned out to be no more willing to part with money than the ones in Alabama. They always pleaded that they were working with a tight budget in a tough year. I knew by then that it was never really about money. The real fight was over priorities, and I'd learned to make children's issues a priority by applying the right pressure in the right places. It took a little over two years, but I got the job done, and we got the money for a new detention center.

Through all this, I kept in close touch with Howard Mandell, who continued to work incredibly hard without my help. I know Howard got some help from the Southern Poverty Law Center, but mostly he paid the bills out of his pocket. With all the exhibits, depositions, and other documents, the file in the Player case alone eventually swelled to some 100,000 pages. I guess it took Judge Johnson a while to read through it all, but he finally handed down his ruling in August 1975—and we won. The judge ordered the state to give black children access to the same institutional care that white kids got. He didn't order the private homes to integrate, but he ordered the state to build its own homes if they didn't.

"You should feel good—really, really good," Howard wrote to me. "As a result of your courageous stand and actions, thousands of young black children in Alabama will now have a better chance to succeed in life. You should really be proud of yourself."

I was proud of us both, and I was eager for even more good news about my reinstatement that Howard seemed certain would follow. "Player is victory number 1 for us," he wrote. "I now await victory No. 2—your own case." The news was a long time coming, but the wait seemed worthwhile when it did. Howard sent the ruling to me in April 1976, with a note: "Yes, it is not a mirage. We have been vindicated." A three-judge panel from the Fifth Circuit of the U.S. Court of Appeals had overturned Judge Varner and ruled I could have my old job back, although it left the matter of awarding back pay up to the lower court. By this point, of course, I didn't want my old job back, but I savored the victory so much that I told Howard I'd be willing to go back to Montgomery to work for one day just so I could have the pleasure of resigning.

Unfortunately, I never got the chance. Judge Thetford's attorneys filed an appeal of my appeal, and the entire fifteen-member court agreed to hear it. I still can't understand how this happened, but the majority ruled against me. My gut told me it was because a judge will naturally side with another judge, but what do I know? We filed our last appeal with the U.S. Supreme Court, knowing the chance of getting a hearing there was about on a par with my chance of winning the lottery. Sure enough, we were turned down in April 1977. If I had to pick one of my three federal cases

High Court 4/4/77
Turns Down
Abbott Appeal

WASHINGTON (AP) — The Supreme 1969 suit filed in federal court, a fact that
Court today turned down the appeal of a prompted Thetford to chastise the
former Montgomery County, Ala., youth probation officer and order that no other
official who claims he was fired after fil- lawsuits be filed by that office.
ing a suit to racially integrate child-care

to lose, this was certainly the one I would have chosen, but that didn't make it hurt any less.

LOSING TO MY OLD nemesis Judge Thetford wasn't the only raw spot in my life either. My marriage to Sharon was breaking up. I don't think my court fights or anything related to them had a thing to do with it. We were just very different people who were moving in different directions. We separated, we tried counseling. Then we reconciled and moved into a new house in Coral Springs, just outside of Fort Lauderdale. But in the end, we were divorced. I stayed in Florida with the kids, and she went off to sea with a guy who owned a sailboat. I was used to managing a staff and balancing a budget, but managing a household and balancing groceries as I maneuvered an overflowing cart through the supermarket aisles was a lot tougher than I imagined. I developed a whole new respect for single parents, as I told a reporter when the local paper interviewed me for a Mr. Mom story about single fathers.

Until then, I'd always thought of myself as not only a good parent but an involved parent. I rarely skipped a school function and never missed any of Drew's football games. I always made time for family trips and birthday parties. But when I suddenly found myself alone with the three of them, I realized that I'd become emotionally distant from my children. I'd invested so much emotion in other people's children that I'd cheated my own. I realized that Sharon had been the one who sat up with them when they were sick, who listened to every heartbreak involving a boyfriend or girlfriend, and who transported them to school functions and social events. Now it was all my job, and it was terrifying and wonderful at the same time. I am closer to every one of my children to this day because of that experience.

I started a new job around this time in 1979, as executive

director of a nonprofit group called Child Advocacy Inc., which raised awareness of children's issues such as nutrition, health care, and child abuse. We took on a number of good causes, like getting the state to pay for surgery on a three-year-old boy from a poor family. We also established a local guardian *ad litem* program, which allowed the courts to assign an advocate for abused and abandoned children.

One of Child Advocacy's major accomplishments was leading a community fundraising campaign to build a shelter for homeless teens in Fort Lauderdale, where the famous beachfront Strip was a magnet for runaways from around the nation. News reports had repeatedly spotlighted the sad existence of boys and girls who arrived full of hope for a new life in the Florida sunshine, only to be swept up into prostitution, drugs, and crime. Many of these children had run away from abusive homes or had been abandoned by their parents, but most people saw them as predators rather than as victims, and many worried that building a shelter would only encourage more runaways to show up.

One person who truly understood these children and their predicament was Alcee Hastings, a local juvenile court judge who was later elevated to the federal bench and is now a member of Congress. He and I came up with an idea that was a bit theatrical but highly effective. We invited the county legislative delegation and the media to attend a sort of mock trial in the judge's courtroom. The delegation sat in the jury box, and Judge Hastings took his usual seat up on the bench. With the help of local activist and attorney Norman Kent, we got real children from the streets to come in and take the witness stand. Legislators heard the harsh realities of life on the streets directly from the children who were suffering the consequences. I have always believed that the best way to influence decision-makers is to impact their senses—make them hear, touch, smell, and see the issue. The strategy worked on the legislators gathered in Judge Hastings's courtroom. When they went back to the capital, they came up with the money for the shelter.

In 1981, we began to focus on a new challenge: the under-reported problem of missing children. Back then, you didn't see pictures on milk cartons or hear missing-child alerts on the radio. Worst of all, most police departments treated each case as a strictly local matter. There was no coordination, no sharing of even basic information. Parents of missing children were often told to just sit and wait, while in reality little was being done to find their children. Most people had no inkling of this until a six-year-old boy named Adam Walsh disappeared from a Sears store in Hollywood, Florida, in July 1981.

Adam was watching a video-game demonstration with other kids while his mother looked at lamps in the next department. She came back for him after a few minutes, but he was gone—forever. At first, John and Revé Walsh believed police would do everything possible to find their son, but they soon came to realize how wrong they'd been. Police not only failed to call in sufficient resources to look for Adam, they mishandled evidence and over-looked important leads. It was left to the Walshes themselves to spread the word about their missing son and rouse the public to help look for him. Tragically, Adam's head was discovered more than one hundred miles away in a Vero Beach canal two weeks after he disappeared.

For a long time, the search for Adam's killer was no more fruitful than the search for Adam. The first real break appeared in 1983, when a vagabond roofer and confessed serial killer named Ottis Toole made a startling jailhouse confession to coaxing Adam into his 1971 Cadillac and killing him. From his cell at Union Correctional Institution in Raiford, Florida, Toole wrote John Walsh a letter that is heartbreaking in its taunting cruelty and vulgarity. He demanded five thousand dollars to reveal where he'd buried Adam's body. That letter and details of the crime that Toole revealed in interviews with detectives left little doubt in John's mind that Toole was Adam's killer.

But after declaring the case solved, Hollywood police started to backtrack and express doubts about Toole's guilt. The case went cold, and Toole eventually recanted his confession. Any chance of prosecuting him was lost along with the Cadillac, which was released from the evidence lockup and sold for scrap. Toole died in prison without ever saying more about what happened to Adam.

Yet John persevered, publicly pressing the case against Toole. It took twenty-five years, but on December 16, 2008, Hollywood police officially closed Adam's case after declaring that Ottis Toole was his killer.

JOHN AND REVÉ WALSH are remarkable people. They endured the loss of a child under the most horrifying circumstances. They endured the calloused response of local police, who refused to call in the FBI or even the county sheriff to help find their son. They endured the most public and microscopic inspection of their lives by a press that seemed bent on proving they were responsible for their own child's murder. And after all this, they dedicated themselves to saving other children and parents from the same tortures.

The Walshes created a whirlwind of publicity about the faults in the system that made life far too easy for predators, and they began to lobby for national legislation to correct those faults. I had already begun to look at the possibility of a data-sharing system within Broward County, but our grant was running out. I approached John with the idea that we might be able to work together, and he agreed. John and Revé joined the board of Child Advocacy, and we soon changed the name to the Adam Walsh

Child Resource Center, Inc. I became its national director.

In the years that followed, John and I traveled around the country speaking to legislative groups about the need for reform. We worked together to create model statutes to protect children and carried them from state to state. In the course of our research, we uncovered some truly scary gaps in existing law. For example, in 1984, forty professions in Florida required a federal background check, including doctors, lawyers. Even race track grooms. But you could be a convicted child molester and get a job at a daycare center or as a public school teacher in Florida because no background check was required. We worked together on a proposed law to fix that, which was much easier than getting it passed.

The reason such gaps existed in the first place is that children don't vote, and unlike the insurance industry or the banks, they didn't have a lobby to put pressure on the right people. We had to learn how to do that for them. One of the first lessons we learned was that there was always going to be opposition, even to a common-sense law like one requiring background checks for child-care workers. I remember some heated arguments with officials from teachers unions, for example, who felt insulted by the idea or who didn't want their members to go through the hassle of being fingerprinted.

Our initial publicity efforts built public support, but I knew that random calls or even petitions were easy enough for legislators to ignore. We needed to concentrate on a handful of critical votes. In Florida, as in most states, bills live or die in committees. If they make it to a full vote in either the House or the Senate, they usually pass. So we targeted the key committee members, and we fine-tuned our approach by rallying troops from within those committee members' home districts. I enlisted help from civic groups around the state and made postcards for each group to pass out to its members in the key districts. The message to our legislative targets was short and powerful, urging support for the bill and adding: "I live and vote in your district. You can count on my continued support only if you support this bill." The message got through loud and clear. The bill passed, and the governor signed it with considerable fanfare.

I also helped John take on some tough cases that drew national publicity, including the disappearance of a twenty-year-old University of Florida student. Tiffany Sessions left her Gainesville apartment at 4 p.m. on February 9, 1989, and never returned. Her father, Patrick, used his professional marketing experience to engineer a search and publicity campaign of Walsh-like proportions. He posted a $75,000 reward, mailed 30,000 fliers, and set up a toll-free number to receive tips. John offered to help, and the two of us went to Patrick's house. I listened as John offered a wealth of advice on how to proceed with the search, handle the media, and, most important, how to stay healthy while bearing up under the pressure. One of the friends at Patrick's house was Dan Marino, quarterback of the Miami Dolphins. Dan offered to ask his friend Bob Costas to discuss Tiffany's case on his nationally syndicated radio show. Costas agreed to have Dan on the show, and I went along to help with questions about missing persons. Dan and I flew off to New York together and taped the show, which led to even more publicity about Tiffany's plight. Unfortunately, she has never been found.

John and I got some very important work done on behalf of America's children. In the process, I was exposed to a different side of the criminal justice system, working to help victims. John is still an amazingly energetic advocate on behalf of all victims of crime, as anyone who has seen *America's Most Wanted* knows. I also remain passionate, but I'm not quite so energetic. I had reached my fifties by the time the Adam Walsh Center merged with the National Center for Missing and Exploited Children in 1990. My position was eliminated, and I decided to look for an opportunity closer to home that didn't demand constant travel. I found it with the Palm Beach County Division of Victim Services.

I was settling into my new routine in midsummer of 1990, when a letter arrived from the California public defender's office in Los Angeles. The first sentence just about knocked me out of my chair:

> I am writing to inquire if you would be available to act as an expert witness regarding conditions at the Alabama Industrial School for Negro Children at Mt. Meigs.

8

Mt. Meigs, the Rest of the Story

Therene Powell was the lawyer for convicted murderer Jesse James Andrews, who was awaiting execution on California's death row. Andrews had served time at Mt. Meigs as a teenager, and Powell believed his experience there might hold the key to a successful appeal. She wrote to me because she thought I could help her. I was intrigued, but I wanted to know more before I agreed to get involved.

What I learned about the early life of Jesse Andrews sounded like the story of a hundred boys I'd counseled back in Montgomery. The grandfather who was raising him died, and Jesse bounced from home to home, getting into minor scrapes along the way. At thirteen, he went along on a joy ride with an older boy and got caught in a stolen car. A juvenile court judge in Mobile declared him incorrigible and sent him to Mt. Meigs. Soon after his release, Andrews drove the getaway car in a robbery that ended in the shooting death of a store clerk. It was the first of several violent crimes that introduced him to Alabama's adult prison system.

Listening to Andrews's account of his time at Mt. Meigs, Powell and his other lawyers became convinced the brutality he saw and experienced there helped turn him into a career criminal. They dug deeper and discovered my long-ago lawsuit.

Before I agreed to help, I wanted to know more about what I'd be getting into. I was concerned that I'd have to fly to California for various hearings and possibly even a new trial. Also, frankly, the facts of the case were horrifying.

Andrews and an accomplice were accused of murdering three people on December 9, 1979. Someone came knocking at the Los Angeles apartment of a man named Preston Wheeler, looking to rob him. Wheeler made the fatal mistake of opening the door. When police arrived later that night, they found Wheeler's bloody body in the living room. He'd been beaten, stabbed six times in the chest, and shot in the neck at close range.

Patrice Brandon, Wheeler's girlfriend, was found dead in the kitchen, where she'd been raped and then strangled with a coat hanger. A neighbor, Ronald Chism, apparently heard the commotion and came knocking, too. He was strangled for his trouble. The police found his body in the bathroom.

Two men were eventually arrested, Charles Sanders and Jesse Andrews. Sanders made a bargain with prosecutors. He was spared the death penalty in return for his testimony. On the witness stand, he blamed Andrews for each of the killings, the rape, and even for the idea of robbing the place. The jury believed him. Sanders was sentenced to a prison term of seventeen years to life. Andrews was sentenced to die in the gas chamber.

I told Powell I would testify about the conditions at Mt. Meigs but would not get involved in the mitigation of the sentence. Co-counsel Billie Jan Goldstein explained that the appeal would not affect Andrews's conviction, just the death sentence. Even that didn't set my mind at ease because I've always supported the death penalty, but she assured me that my testimony would be limited to what I knew about Mt. Meigs—and I could make my statement under oath in Florida to be entered into the record in California. That, most likely, would be the end of my involvement.

The more I learned, the more intrigued I became. The public defender's office was tracking down a number of men who'd been locked up with Andrews in various institutions, including some who'd been incarcerated at Mt. Meigs. The office had also contacted Ira De Ment, who agreed to give a deposition. This strange case from so far away suddenly presented the opportunity to find out more about what really happened at Mt. Meigs from people who were now living with the consequences. I signed the witness form and then started reopening my dusty boxes of old legal papers and notes to refresh my memory.

Over the next couple of years, California investigators contacted nearly forty men who had done time with Andrews in Alabama. All but two or three had also been incarcerated at Mt. Meigs. The Mt. Meigs alumni had followed a strikingly similar route after their release, committing violent crimes that led them to adult prison. Two were on death row, and several others were doing life terms for crimes such as murder and manslaughter.

The numbers alone showed we had been right: Mt. Meigs wasn't a school at all. It was a factory that manufactured criminals, using children as raw material. The depositions in the Andrews case detailed the unrelenting pain and punishment that erased from these children any sense of hope or belief in the decency of human beings. Testimony from one after another made clear that the only choice allowed at Mt. Meigs was to become a victim or to prey on others. Neither path could possibly lead to a normal, productive life.

Consider these examples from statements submitted in the Andrews case:

- Field work was "often accompanied by severe beatings, given for the most minor infractions." Boys were beaten if they failed to pick enough cotton in a day to fill a bag six feet long, "the size of a bed sheet." They were also beaten if they left any seeds or blades of grass in the cotton.

- Guards beat boys even before the day's work began as a lesson to other boys. The beatings were often so severe that the victims bled, "and then the guards would not permit the boys to wipe the blood off."

- Boys were forced to run miles through the fields. If a boy collapsed from exhaustion, "he would be beaten by guards who would accuse the boy of faking illness."
- The choir director beat boys for hitting a wrong note.
- Other punishments could be even worse than beatings: "Some of us was forced to drink from the sewer."
- Violence among the boys was not only tolerated but encouraged by the staff. One former inmate testified that a boy who complained about another would be told by guards to "either kill him or be his whore." Any boy who was challenged to a fight had to accept or be beaten by the guards. If a boy lost a fight, "he would be forced to submit to sex with the boy that beat him, and anyone else who wanted him."

Some of the witness statements were more detailed than others, but it's the similarities that stand out. For example, a number recalled that the beating sticks wielded by the guards were all called "John Henry." Boys were warned not to cry or complain while being hit or the beatings would continue until they were quiet. They were permitted to say nothing except, "Thank you, John Henry."

Several testified that E. B. Holloway, the school's superintendent, frequently beat the students. Once, Holloway caught a boy smoking and made him drop his pants in the mess hall in front of the others. Then Holloway paddled him repeatedly until the boy bled, the witness testified.

Another supervisor, Tom Glover, was described in sadistic terms in several statements. He'd poke a hole in the ground, then order a student to take his pants off and lie down with his penis in the hole. He'd insist the boy then lie still for a beating, the inmates said. If a boy moved, one testified, "you get extra licks.

So the average guy try to stay there and just take them licks. He hitting you as hard as he can."

A guard identified only as Mr. Jim used a bullwhip to keep boys in line. One former inmate said he saw Mr. Jim whip Jesse Andrews, one of many instances of abuse that Andrews endured, according to witnesses.

Many former inmates spoke of filth everywhere at Mt. Meigs— in the dorms, the bathrooms, the mess hall. Others described constant hunger or food that was spoiled and insect-infested. One said the children became so desperate they picked corn out of cow manure in the fields and ate it.

The threat of rape was constant, especially for the younger students. Boys in the fields would be dragged off into the woods by supervisors. Those supervisors were often older students called "charge boys," who had learned to escape punishment by inflicting it on others. The main qualification for being a charge boy was the ability to fight—and win. If a guy was in charge and you wanted the position, you fought him, one inmate testified. "It was like gladiators. It was for sport."

Owners of nearby farms were referred to as "neighborhood watchmen," because they were expected to call the school if they spotted runaways. In return for their vigilance, they could call over any time for boys to work their fields. The depositions bolstered what Ira and I had heard from others: some of these neighboring farms belonged to the school's trustees, who exploited the children for free labor.

Boys were warned that anyone who tried to escape would be shot, and several testified they believed it had happened, although none had first-hand knowledge of it. Many tried to escape anyway. One told of being so desperate he slipped under an eighteen-wheeler and clung to the truck's spare tire until it stopped in Mobile, nearly two hundred miles away.

Regardless of whether children were shot, some died of abuse or neglect. William J. Samford II, then counsel for the Alabama Department of Youth Services, told California investigators "there were many deaths [at Mt. Meigs] from illness and malnutrition in the sixties and previously."

One former inmate testified he'd been put in charge of medical care at Mt. Meigs when the school nurse quit. He was fifteen years old at the time. His duties included giving other students tetanus shots and bandaging wounds. "I have went as far as to stitch a few peoples up," he said.

That same inmate summed up the school as "a little slave camp . . . they work you to death and beat your ass."

Even now, I get emotional reading these depositions. These victims were children placed in the state's care by a court of law. I don't have words to describe a place that would do such things to them, but Ira De Ment did. One of the attorneys in the Andrews case asked him what it was about our lawsuit that justified the intervention of the federal government. He replied, "The absolute denial of basic and fundamental human rights to Negro children who were incarcerated in a concentration camp at Mt. Meigs, Alabama."

The California public defender's office also presented expert testimony that the conditions at Mt. Meigs in the 1960s were similar to conditions at adult prisons that had been proven to provoke violent reactions among former inmates. They could not find any study showing the result of such conditions in reform schools, because no one had ever seen such conditions at any school except Mt. Meigs, according to Donald J. Ayoob, who took over the case as Andrews's public defender for the death-penalty appeal.

At least two defendants from other states have since filed similar appeals based on their experiences at segregated reform schools. Both schools were shown to be quite rough, Ayoob said, but "as bad as the Louisiana and Tennessee places were, they didn't hold a candle to Mt. Meigs." His investigation in the Andrews case left Ayoob with the same indelible impression of Mt. Meigs that our lawsuit had left on Ira and me. "It was a slave labor camp," he said.

Judging by the testimony, Jesse Andrews suffered badly. He was smaller than most, so he was a perpetual whipping boy. One inmate told investigators he saw Andrews beaten three to four times a week. "He believes the guards beat Jesse so badly because they wanted him to behave like an animal, and Jesse wanted to behave like a man," the investigator wrote. "The guards snatched away and stripped Jesse of his pride, dignity and principles. Jesse left Mt. Meigs a very different boy."

In the end, none of this helped the public defender's case. The argument for Andrews's appeal was basically this: His original trial lawyer should have presented testimony about Mt. Meigs because the jury might have considered it a mitigating factor and rejected the death penalty. The California Supreme Court turned down that appeal in August 2002. The majority ruled that introducing such testimony could have opened the door for the prosecution to present even more damaging evidence about Andrews's criminal past.

As of 2012, Jesse Andrews remained on death row.

9

A Call for Help

As coordinator of victim services for Palm Beach County, I had about twenty counselors working for me. Most had more experience than I did helping people manage the aftershocks that victims experience when they've been beaten, robbed, or worse.

Some people need information about how to file a police report. Others need counseling to get through the trauma. And some just need to know that somebody understands what they're going through. I knew I couldn't be an effective supervisor unless I'd been through all of this, so I put myself on the on-call list from day one. I insisted on getting the whole range of experience, including rape cases, which our office had assigned only to women counselors until then.

Nothing about the first ten or twelve rape cases I handled prepared me for the call that came to my home at 9:30 a.m. Saturday, March 30, 1991. It was from a woman who identified herself only as Patti. She had reported being raped the night before, and the police gave her my phone number. She told me her attacker was someone well-known, and she was afraid he might hurt her again. I asked her to meet me at the sheriff's department, where she'd be safe. She had to pick up her two-year-old daughter first, so it was about 11 a.m. by the time we met there. I hadn't asked for a description, but I knew her the moment she got out of her car: she was shaking uncontrollably.

When I first walked toward her, she jumped back. "No," she

said. I kept my distance as we went to the room reserved for sexual assault victims. Patti was shaking the whole time we talked. She continued to shake when a detective joined us, and kept on shaking when we went together to a nearby hospital. She shook that whole day, but I gained her trust. She insisted that I stay with her while she was examined and then asked me to drive her home.

No one who saw Patricia Bowman that day, or heard the fear in her voice, could possibly doubt the story she told me: she had been raped the night before by William Kennedy Smith on the beach behind the Kennedy estate on Palm Beach.

The basic events of the evening were undisputed. Patti, then twenty-nine, had gone out for dinner and drinks with friends. She came face to face with Smith, a Georgetown University medical student on Easter break, while on her way to the restroom. He introduced himself and took her to his table to meet his dinner companions—his cousin Patrick and his Uncle Ted. Patti and Willie, as his friends called him, danced until closing time. His uncle and cousin were gone by then, so Patti offered to drive him home.

Patti had no qualms about going home with a man she didn't know because the home was something of a historical landmark, the mansion known as the second White House when Willie's Uncle Jack was president. She also knew they'd have plenty of company, including one of the most respected members of the United States Senate.

Patti and Willie ducked out for a moonlight stroll along the secluded beach. Willie suggested a swim, but Patti thought it was too chilly—and besides, it was getting late. This is where accounts began to seriously diverge. Willie said Patti lingered at the water's edge long enough to engage in consensual sex. Patti said she started to head back to the house when Willie tackled her and then raped her. Either way, she got back to the house and phoned her friends to come and get her. She told them the same story she told me. It was a story the entire nation heard and dissected in the months that followed, as Patti was forced to testify in front of a nationwide television audience. Millions came to know her as the woman behind the blue dot, TV's modest attempt to conceal her face while she testified.

In truth, Patti had been stripped of her privacy the moment the story hit the press. Most papers followed convention—and Florida law—by withholding her name from their stories, but the reporters all knew who she was. The calls started almost immediately, followed by knocks at the door. TV trucks parked along the block outside her house, and camera crews peered through the windows. One of the tabloids offered her $100,000 to talk. I don't have to guess how terrified she was by all this, because she told me.

I told Patti to call me at home any time, and she didn't hesitate to do so. Sometimes she asked for my advice, and sometimes she just wanted to talk. Other times she needed more direct assistance just getting in and out of her home past the press. One day when I showed up to escort her to a court hearing, I actually saw photographers perched in the trees out front. I pulled my car into the garage and shut the door behind me. When I pulled out a few minutes later, the photographers went into a frenzy of clicking until they saw that I was alone in the car. What they didn't know was that Patti was in the trunk.

Over and over she told me how scared she was. She said Willie Smith told her that night on the beach that no one would ever believe her, and she worried that he was right. She also worried that he was a powerful man from a powerful family. She called me late one night because she was afraid to go to bed; she thought someone might break into her house and hurt her.

I tried to reassure Patti that she was physically safe, and I was certain she was. I couldn't give her much reassurance about the media. No one was surprised when a splashy tabloid called the *Globe* defied the law and printed her full name, but I was stunned that the *New York Times* and a major TV network did, too. It was as though the news media had decided to punish Patti for not cooperating, or maybe for daring to accuse a Kennedy of such an awful thing.

Patti didn't deserve that. No rape victim deserves that. I knew from experience that all crimes leave their marks on victims, but rape is in a category by itself. Everyone today agrees that rape victims shouldn't be stigmatized, but the fact is they are stigmatized—and rapists know that. It's one of the powerful weapons rapists hold over women: you can't tell anyone what happened without hurting yourself even more. Women have always been afraid to come forward, and the way Patti was treated could only make that even harder. I heard all the arguments about freedom of the press and the public's right to know. They don't mean a thing to a woman who's been brutalized by an attacker, and then brutalized again by the media.

The controversy over identifying Patti spawned its own court case when prosecutors filed charges against the *Globe*. Unfortunately, the result was that the state law protecting rape victims' names from publication was declared unconstitutional. I wasn't surprised, but I was angry. I wrote an opinion piece for the *Palm Beach Post* noting that our office had seen a marked drop in rape reports after Patti's name was published, and that other centers around the country had seen the same.

"The first question now asked by victims is whether their identity is going to be made public," I wrote. "We can tell them only that we will not release personal information about them and hope that the media also will protect their identity."

I'm happy to say that responsible members of the media,

Palm Beach Post 5-26-91

Prosecute namers of rape victims: It's the law

By DENNY ABBOTT

On May 1, George McEvoy of The Palm Beach Post wrote a column supporting the public identity of rape victims, and on May 11, The Post published an editorial that stated that Palm Beach County State Attorney David Bludworth should not prosecute a tabloid based in Boca Raton, The Globe, for publishing a rape victim's name and photograph.

The Palm Beach County Victim Services office feels very strongly that the identity of rape victims should remain confidential. Rape is the most violent individual violation of a person's privacy and dignity. Public exposure of a rape victim is a societal invasion of a person's privacy and constitutes a second victimization. Because the healing process for a rape victim is hastened by a return to normalcy as soon as possible, public identification makes a speedy recovery virtually impossible.

Most victims feel ashamed and fearful if their identity is known.

Both stranger rape and acquaintance rape are still very much misunderstood by the general public. Most victims feel ashamed and fearful that they will be ostracized by the general community if their identity is known. They are right. We as victim advocates need to do a better job of public education. The tide will turn if we can raise the level of awareness, encourage reporting, treat victims with dignity and respect, and treat offenders for what they are — criminals.

Mr. McEvoy correctly states that in the alleged assault at the Kennedy estate, the accused was unfairly victimized by the press prior to the filing of formal charges. Naming the victim, however, will not achieve equity and fairness but will only make a bad situation worse.

There should be serious discussion about protecting the identity of the accused, at least until probable cause has been established and formal charges filed.

The Post also feels that charges should not be brought against the media for violating Florida law. Perhaps the statute is flawed, but that is for appellate courts to decide, not newspapers. We have already spoken to legal experts, who are drafting a model statute that should withstand legal review. Constitutional rights, such as the First Amendment, are not absolute. If so, there would be no limitations for citizens to bear arms under any conditions. Laws should reflect the will of the people. Eighty percent, or more, of Americans believe in the anonymity of rape victims.

We believe that a failure to prosecute the media would result in fewer reports of sexual assault and an increase in sexual crimes. Rape is the most underreported crime in our society, with only about one in 10 being reported. We are experiencing an increase in sexual assaults across the country, with a dramatic increase in Florida of 9 percent over last year. Public identification already has had a chilling effect on local reporting of sexual as-

sault, and The Post reported national evidence of fewer reports in an editorial on May 16.

It shouldn't be a surprise that The Post is no friend to victims of crime. A few years ago, The Post opposed the state constitutional amendment for victims. It is a simple recognition that victims have rights in our criminal justice process. (Editor's note: The Post opposed the amendment because "it isn't needed to establish many victims' rights in Florida and would be unlikely to affect many criminal justice outcomes.") Fortunately, more than 90 percent of Florida voters did not agree with The Post and approved the amendment.

If the decisionmakers at The Post, or members of their families, are victimized by crime, I'd bet they would see things differently.

■

Denny Abbott, coordinator of the Palm Beach County Victim Services, counseled the victim in the William Kennedy Smith rape case. He wrote this article for The Palm Beach Post.

along with public opinion, have remained on the right side of the issue. Probably the only good thing to come out of the intense media coverage of Patti's case was a heightened awareness of the challenges that all crime victims face. I must have answered calls from fifty or sixty reporters, many of whom knew nothing about victim services and the role we play in helping people. I took the opportunity to educate the public about how crime victims are treated—and sometimes, mistreated.

My continuing role as Patti's counselor gave me a unique vantage point for what was probably the most highly publicized trial since the Lindbergh kidnapping back in the 1930s. I almost took the stand, and I'm sorry I didn't. I was on the witness list, but I was never called to testify. I think I could have helped Patti's case, but I'm even more disappointed that prosecutors ignored my advice. I urged them to have an expert witness testify about what a rapist looks like. I knew the defense would take advantage of the common misconception that a rapist has to be some guy in a trench coat loitering in the shadows. I wanted someone to testify that rapists can look like anyone, even like a clean-cut medical student. It wasn't until near the end of the trial that the prosecution realized I was right and tried to add another witness, but Judge Mary Lupo ruled that it was too late.

I kept the notes from my conversations with Patti leading up to the trial. I still respect her privacy, so I won't share all her thoughts, but I can tell you that she asked repeatedly how I thought the trial would turn out. We both knew she'd be a great and sympathetic witness, but we also knew Smith would be cool and well-prepared. His attorney, Roy Black, was just about the best in the business. I really believed the difference would come down to the evidence—specifically, the evidence that this was not the first time Smith had faced such accusations. Investigators had found three other women who said Smith had suddenly turned violent and raped them. Unlike Patti, none had filed charges. Each said she was intimidated by the Kennedy name and by Smith's taunting assurance that no one would believe her.

From my notes:

> Dec. 1—I called Patti at home on the eve of the trial just to let her know I was thinking of her. She again asked my opinion of the outcome. I again told her that, in my opinion, the testimony of the other 3 women was crucial.
>
> Dec. 2—Trial starts. Lupo won't let 3 women testify. There goes the case.

Unfortunately for Patti, my assessment was correct. William Kennedy Smith went free, but Patti did not retreat in fear. She stepped out from behind the blue dot and stepped in front of the TV cameras. Patti became an outspoken advocate for other victims, working with victims' rights groups in Florida and elsewhere.

I grew to admire Patti greatly during and after the trial. I could see the pain on her face, I could feel how badly she'd been hurt, but she held up under the most personal and vicious attacks from the defense and the intrusions of the press. She had to put up with innuendo and outright slander that no man would ever have to stand for. Once in mid-trial, I was in a courthouse elevator with some women who were talking about the case. One said Patti got what she deserved because she was out at 2 o'clock in the morning. I couldn't keep quiet. I asked her to tell me at what time, exactly, should the law stop protecting women? Eight o'clock? Ten o'clock? Midnight? They all immediately understood the absurdity of blaming the victim. I wish everyone could.

After the verdict came in, I heard one of the jurors tell a TV reporter that Smith didn't look like a rapist. It was one of those times when there's no satisfaction at all in knowing you were right.

10

Hindsight

I t's hard for me to believe that most of my life has passed since I left Alabama. I've had a number of different careers over the subsequent years: I ran a public health clinic, and I worked at an agency that helped the chronically unemployed find jobs. I was the director of two nonprofit agencies, Child Advocacy and the Adam Walsh Child Resource Center; coordinator of Victim Services for Palm Beach County, Florida (I wrote legislation that became Florida law); regional administrator for the Florida Department of Labor; and consultant for the South Florida Water Management District.

I'm proud of everything I've accomplished, but I'm proudest of the nearly thirty years I devoted to helping children. I think I can truly say I never turned my back on a child in trouble. I still don't know how anyone can. If there's anything I tried to impress on my own children, it's that we have a moral duty to protect those who can't protect themselves. We have to speak for them, act for them, and sometimes fight for them.

Some of the details of my many fights are getting a little hazy, but just about everyone I asked for help in telling this story was eager to talk. Unfortunately, many of the key figures, including my parents, are long gone.

Judge Thetford died in August 1977, just four months after the Supreme Court refused to consider my case against him. He was sixty-four years old.

Judge Frank Johnson died in 1999, and Judge Robert Varner died 2006.

George Wallace, who left his imprint on nearly everything in Alabama, was shot and permanently disabled while campaigning for president in 1972. He ran for governor again ten years later, campaigning in his wheelchair. The man who vowed to defend segregation forever claimed to have had a change of heart and asked black people across Alabama to support him. Many did, and Wallace won. He remained governor until 1987, and he died in 1998.

Emmett Player, now in his fifties, still lives in rural Alabama. He declined to be interviewed for this book but relayed word through his wife that he depends on disability payments for support.

Howard Mandell was most gracious in lending his advice and recollections to this project. He remained in Montgomery for many years, continuing to fight for the people who needed him. In a curious role reversal, the former thorn in the city's side became Montgomery's city attorney in 2000, when a new mayor asked him to help show that the city had changed. Two years later, he set out on a very different path. He quit the law and entered the Jewish Theological Seminary in New York. Today, he is Rabbi Howard Mandell.

Ira De Ment was appointed federal judge by President George H. W. Bush in 1992, and he remained on the job as active and then senior judge until his death in 2011. His rulings were fiercely independent, as you'd expect of a judge who calls himself "a progressive populist." He angered fundamentalists by striking down a state law that would have allowed non-sectarian prayer in schools, and he angered gay activists by turning down a challenge to Alabama's anti-sodomy statute.

Judge De Ment was one of the first people I went to see when my wife, Adele, and I drove back to Montgomery in 2006. Although obviously in great discomfort from severe back pain that troubled him in his later years, he met with us in his chambers and eagerly recounted his involvement in the Mt. Meigs battle. In short order, the two of us started swapping ideas and what-ifs as though it were 1969 again. The only regret he expressed was when I mentioned E. B. Holloway.

"I should have prosecuted him," he said.

"Maybe it's not too late," I suggested.

"There's no statute of limitations on child abuse," he replied.

We both felt the old spark as we looked each other in the eye, but the moment passed—and so had any chance for justice. Holloway, I later learned, had died in February 1976, at age 69.

Looking back, it's sad and depressing to realize that no one was ever charged with a crime for the outrages at Mt. Meigs. No one had to answer to a judge or jury for beating and sexually abusing children and then stealing the food from their plates. The crimes we revealed were shocking, the evidence abundant, and the perpetrators clearly identified. The State of Alabama acknowledged all of it in accepting Judge Johnson's order. Yet no state or local law enforcement agency made any inquiry, much less arrests.

On our trip to Montgomery, we stopped at what is now known as the Mt. Meigs Complex, which includes a drug treatment program, a sex offender program, and an independent living center for youths who need long-term support and counseling. The school at Mt. Meigs is now known as the Wallace School.

We got a tour of the campus from J. Walter Woods Jr., director of the state Department of Youth Services—yes, Alabama finally created one after I left. There were a few newer buildings, but plenty of old ones, too.

I know the worst of the abuses we uncovered at Mt. Meigs ended long ago. All of the state's youth facilities are now staffed by trained professionals, not illiterates and criminals. Kids are no longer routinely beaten by the people who are supposed to look after them. I take real pride in helping to end that. But I also know the reforms that our lawsuits helped bring about weren't all permanent or as complete as we'd hoped they would be.

Way back in 1975, after I had moved to Florida, a friend sent me a clipping from the *Montgomery Advertiser*. The headline: "Will Past Mistakes Continue to Hamper Mt. Meigs School?" The story reported on a state audit showing "slipshod management" along with "incidents of homosexual rape, drug use, gambling, stealing, and fighting" among the students. In the years since, reports have continued to surface about trouble at Mt. Meigs, particularly gang problems. "About 75 percent of the juveniles who go to Mt. Meigs are in gangs," Marshall County District Judge David Evans told the *Gadsden Times* in 1994. "I would say that when they come out, 90 percent are in gangs. I don't want a kid to stay at Mt. Meigs if I can avoid it."

I've learned from experience that it's impossible to sustain a high level of public awareness or involvement in youth issues unless someone or some group makes a real effort to expose problems and shake up the system. I know there are many good people willing to take risks in order to make a difference.

Maybe this book will encourage some to try.